CARE
for the
WORLD

Reflections on Community Ministry

Edited by Erin J. Walter

Skinner House Books
Boston

To everyone trying to answer their call

skinnerhouse.org

Printed in the United States

Text and cover design by Tim Holtz
Cover art: "Underground" by Sean Parker Dennison

print ISBN: 978-1-55896-894-3
eBook ISBN: 978-1-55896-895-0

5 4 3 2 1
26 25 24 23 22

Cataloging-in-Publication data on file with the Library of Congress

Contents

Foreword

Rev. Theresa Ninán Soto

Dorothy Day, who changed the world with her fierce, heart-centered work, once shared the following encouraging words, apt for community ministers today: "The greatest challenge of the day is: how to bring about a revolution of the heart, a revolution which has to start with each one of us."

Community ministers—both ordained and lay—are a living example of the possibility of revolution in each heart, not as individual locations of change but rather as an interdependent chain reaction of transformation.

One of the complexities of community ministry is that the deep treasure of interdependence isn't always obvious. To some, community ministers may appear to be loners. Maybe they are, but only in the same way that one aspen tree is alone. It is a slender tree with bright white bark, brilliant gold foliage in the autumn, quaking leaves, and, below the surface, an extensive and supportive root system.

These trees are always growing. Their extensive, intertwined roots make the entire aspen forest—called a clone—strong. The oldest known clone grows in the Fishlake National Forest in Utah. The clone is over eighty thousand years old and weighs more than 6,600 pounds. The history of community ministry, the significance of ministry outside congregations as people engage with it today, is no less substantial.

Joseph Tuckerman is regarded as the first known Unitarian Universalist community minister. He said, "These effects [of witnessing suffering or need of others] . . . demonstrate not only that God has made us for one another but that, in an important sense, he has made each one of us for the whole of our species."

For both Day and Tuckerman, that reach among and between others to cause transformation and relieve suffering called them forward into leadership and ministry. Of course, there are other strong calls to enter into relationship with the people in community and in the wider world. A variety of calls bring community ministers to their respective labors of love, each of us for the whole.

Tuckerman's words also echo the story of the aspen forest, or clone. Each tree is necessary for the whole clone to thrive. Every time there is one less offering roots and connecting to the larger organism, the entire clone becomes weaker. And just because they look like single trees doesn't mean they are.

A Blessing for Community Ministry

You are a house of worship.
(Or an aspen.)
Your body, your spirit, are the
ever-growing aliveness for which
the world is calling. Sometimes your
leaves may quake. It's understandable.
The world, no, wait, your neighbors and
kin are in distress. And the bark on your
trunk may feel thin when storms come, wind
pushing and pulling at the very same time.
But beneath, there is the part of you that is
always greening. Deeper still, the roots that
keep you connected, alone and together. Our
roots entwine and tangle. They nourish. They
hold steady. We accept that we are individuals.
A blessing, but we can also embody the
certainty of aspen trees, so connected that they
become a marker of that which cannot be
destroyed, but instead remains, regenerates,
and restores.

Introduction

Rev. Erin J. Walter

I took my first class at Meadville Lombard Theological School in 2010, on a cold January weekend on the South Side of Chicago. I was the mother of a newborn and the literacy director of rapidly growing social entrepreneurship Open Books, and I was uncertain what I was getting myself into with seminary.

I had not enrolled at Meadville officially; I wouldn't do so for another four years. Still, I will never forget the title of that first seminary course: Ministry in a Post-Denominational Age. As a lifelong Unitarian Universalist, to say I was suspicious of the phrase *post-denominational* would be an understatement. (Here I was at one of our denomination's two proud seminaries, and it sounded like we might be ditching the denomination!)

I was there—I am still here—for UU ministry. The Rev. Dr. Lee Barker, Meadville's president at the time and a contributor to this book, taught the class and quickly helped me see that I was confusing *post-denominational* with *nondenominational*. The class was about training us to serve in the wider world, not solely within church walls. We learned about creative UU ministries such as The Sanctuaries, a spiritual arts-activist organization in Washington, DC, which you'll hear about later in this book, and Sacred Fire intentional communities in North Carolina.

During that seed-planting weekend in my life, I most remember two things Lee said to our class:

What is your ministry? You already have one,
and,
Would you still do Unitarian Universalist ministry if the denomination name wasn't part of it?

I knew the answer to the first question. Being a director of Open Books was a huge part of what was calling me into ministry. My experiences recruiting, inspiring, training, and mobilizing literacy volunteers across Chicago's diverse but segregated neighborhoods; hiring and coaching staff; writing literacy curriculum; and more all felt like a ministry to me. I was finding my voice and rooting my professional life in my UU principles and passion for antiracism/ antioppression work, whether I could put my finger on that at the time or not.

I wasn't quite sure about Lee's second question, though. Would I want to go through all the toil and trouble of seminary, only to do work that was unidentifiable as UU ministry?

It took me years, but by the time I was ordained, I knew my answer was a resounding *yes.*

I believe this book is needed because community ministry is growing and often not very well understood. Nonprofit work, justice-movement leadership, entrepreneurial ministry, and other forms of community ministry in this collection are still considered radical or simply not remembered as ministry by many in our denomination, let alone the wider world. We need this book because when most ministers say *minister,* we still mean *church minister.* Most community ministers are thought to be hospital or military chaplains, and most people haven't much clue what a community minister is in the first place.

With this book, I sought a window into a variety of community ministries. I found myself reflecting on my own definitions of community ministry and preconceived notions about ministry as a whole.

I kept coming back to the UU Society of Community Ministries' definition:

> Community ministry addresses the social and spiritual needs of people and organizations outside the direct care of congregations. The Unitarian Universalist Society for Community Ministries (UUSCM) is a Unitarian Universalist movement of lay ministers & ordained clergy committed to promoting a broad spectrum of healing and social justice ministries. . . . Community Ministers may be Chaplains, Pastoral Counselors, Spiritual Directors, University or Theological School Faculty, Social Justice Activists, Denominational Officials, or practitioners of a wide range of other activities.

Care for the World aims to inspire all readers to live a spirited, purposeful life, rooting their daily work in their deepest values and faith. I hope these essays will support seminarians and religious professionals who might be in (or considering) community ministry. Without visibility for the critical, sacred work of community ministry, many potential leaders may not hear or consider answering their call.

In my invitations to contributing colleagues, I asked them to think about the following questions:

+ How do you live your UU faith through work in a nonprofit, justice movement, seminary, entrepreneurial ministry, or beyond?
+ What have you learned from that work that you want others to know?
+ What encouragement, advice, or warnings would you give to those considering a call outside the parish?

✦ What is one unforgettable story or experience from your work?

✦ How does community ministry lead our faith?

A common thread for many in community ministry is the sense of being maxed out, whether by the deep and constant need for anti-racism and anti-oppression organizing, by the challenge of working multiple contract jobs to pay the bills in a capitalist society, or other demands on time, mind, and spirit. I didn't want that reality to limit diverse insight and lived experiences in the book, so I conducted some short Q&A discussions that are included here (mostly with folks who could not carve out time to write a chapter), along with the longer-form essays. I consider it a spiritual practice to gratefully receive each person's unique capacity and contribution as gifts to the greater whole—a paradigm shift in pursuit of equity and liberation, and in celebration of what we can each offer Unitarian Universalism and the world.

The time is ripe for these stories. Community ministry is the fastest-growing type of ministry in our faith, and many ministers are bivocational, serving in some combination of parish and community work or finding creative ways to live their calling. One of my favorite examples is Mr. Rogers, who many are just now realizing was an ordained minister. The popular 2018 documentary *Won't You Be My Neighbor?* explored how his show, *Mister Rogers' Neighborhood*, was an expression of his calling. What new or creative expression of your calling could you undertake to change the world?

"Life is messy, full of uncertainty, and often unfair. And somehow we find meaning in these bleak and difficult places," chaplain Kathy Riegelman wrote in *The Call to Care*. You don't have to work in a hospital to experience that. Rev. Barker, who taught that first post-denominational seminary class of mine, wrote this about his transition from twenty-five years of parish ministry to his role as seminary president.

At the time, I had no doubt that my new position would be administrative in nature. What I did not understand is that the skills I would draw upon would be ministerial at their core, and I did not understand how spiritually nurturing such a position could be. Over the years, I have heard it expressed any number of times that moving out of the parish removes one from the 'action' of ministry. I have found the opposite to be true. The stakes are just as high, the ministry is necessary, and the faith is well-served.

My service as an interfaith chaplain and nonprofit director of the YMCA of Austin, which began with my ordination in 2017 and ended with pandemic cutbacks in 2020, was some of the most profound, challenging, joyful, and deeply ministerial work of my life. Since then, my path of community ministry has included virtual ministry and music to more than one hundred congregations from Florida to Canada, spiritual dance classes led over Zoom for people around the world, congregational coaching with Beloved Conversations (The Fahs Collaborative's program for racial justice as a spiritual practice), and spreading UU-centric messages through the music of my rock band, Parker Woodland.

In November 2021, I took on the role of acting executive director of the Texas Unitarian Universalist Justice Ministry, one of our denomination's many statewide-action networks. The path of community ministry has provided me some flexibility to answer my call in varied and creative ways, while also having some flexibility for the needs of my marriage and motherhood. Community ministry, like parish ministry, comes with evolving challenges as well.

In the essays and Q&As of this book, you'll hear from leaders who are in the thick of this work—with Black Lives of UU, climate justice, spiritual direction, our seminaries, denominational-justice organizations, and so much more. As diverse as community ministry is, we cannot cover anywhere near everything in these essays, but the writers and I hope to offer you a rich glimpse into this world and an invitation to delve deeper where you find yourself curious. I encourage you to skip around as the spirit moves you; if you're most intrigued by how tax accounting is ministry, by all means start with Rev. Christian Schmidt's chapter. I do hope you'll reach each chapter and Q&A eventually, in whatever order, because there are such sparkly nuggets of wisdom and inspiration in each one, even if you never plan to join the military (like Rev. Azande Sasa) or start your own UU-centric garage rock band at midlife (like me).

I welcome you to this book and to the spiritual growth happening in our denomination and beyond. If you are a community minister of any stripe, I hope you feel seen by this book. I hope you find in it sources of hope, as well as acknowledgments of the great challenges and hurdles we face within our denomination and beyond.

If this topic is new to you, I am especially grateful you are here and reading. The world needs all of us to show up, every day, with a vision of the Beloved Community, no matter what we do. We need role models—not glossy superheroes or ministers on shaky pedestals but realistic, struggle-and-all role models. We need examples of mission-driven work, whether we are computer programmers or dance teachers, CEOs or domestic workers, stay-at-home parents or full-time volunteers. If you don't quite find the ministry you're looking for here, may *you* create that ministry and write that book. I would love to read it.

Lastly, let me say this: the Unitarian Universalist church is my home. I love it and its ministers and congregations with all my heart.

Sundays nourish and sustain me for the service and mission of the whole week. And I know that the work of our faith will never get done if we leave it to the church alone. We need everyone to claim a piece of community ministry. May each of us represent our faith in the world and advocate for collective liberation every day, in our way, everywhere we go.

Abolitionist Community Ministries in the Age of Mass Incarceration

Rev. Jason Lydon

"I am thankful for the breath in my lungs, the food in my belly, the love of my family, and the care offered to me by people I know and those I do not."

I started my prayer with these words each night as I lay on my top bunk at the Fort Devens federal prison in Massachusetts. In 2003, I was sentenced to six months in prison for taking part in a symbolic act of civil disobedience. I joined nearly one hundred others in trespassing on a military base, intending to raise awareness about US foreign policy in Latin America. We were part of a decades-long movement to close down the United States Army School of the Americas, a training school for soldiers, police officers, and paramilitary leaders. During my incarceration, I deepened my faith and commitment to Unitarian Universalism; my faith had called me to the action that got me locked up in the first place. While incarcerated, surrounded by people who had been victimized by the criminal legal

Rev. Jason Lydon (he/him) grew up as a Unitarian Universalist and entered ministry through the powerful youth movement of the late 90s. Having been introduced to collective liberation work through church conferences, Jason has dedicated his ministries to ending systemic oppression and building up movements for freedom.

system, my connection to a Universalism—a theology that rejects punishment as salvific—grew stronger.

I was twenty years old when I was released from prison. Unlike the far majority of people who spend time in prison, I was released with a job waiting for me, working as a Young Religious Unitarian Universalist (YRUU) programs specialist at the Unitarian Universalist Association in Boston (white privilege leads to very material benefits). I had dropped out of college when I began my prison sentence, and now had the opportunity to serve the young people in our faith in a position focused on developing and implementing antiracist programming for UU youth ages fourteen to twenty.

Working in the Youth Office was an immense privilege and a healing space to be in after six months that included sexual violence by prison staff, forty-five days in solitary confinement, threats of murder by white supremacists, and a terrifying flight on "con air." Throughout this year in UUA youth ministry, I wrote letters back and forth with the friends I'd left behind in prison. We wrote about things we were too afraid to talk about in person: two of the people I wrote with came out as gay, one as HIV positive. I reached out to a number of national LGBTQ+ organizations to share about my experiences of violence, my friend's experience of being denied care, the use of queer-segregated cells in Georgia. I sought support and was informed that "criminal justice issues are not our priority right now." Filled with anger and frustration, I started writing with more queer prisoners, trying to figure out who was doing work to challenge the harms of this racist, homophobic, transmisogynistic system.

I wanted to dedicate my time to our faith and to challenging the violence of the prison industrial complex. I wanted to learn more, act strategically, and get people free. While working as a nanny, I was presented with an opportunity to serve as the congregational director—the minister, essentially—at the Community Church of

Boston, a congregation of older adults who came together because of a shared political vision more than a shared spiritual journey. They were looking for a community organizer with a faith background to take on pastoral, community, and administrative responsibilities at the church. They did not have significant financial resources and therefore had limited options within the formal Unitarian Universalist ministerial search process. After an extensive in-person interview process, we decided to take a risk on each other with a yearlong contract. While this was formerly a parish-focused ministry, one of the congregation's greatest desires was for me to represent and connect them to social-justice struggles within the city of Boston and beyond. It felt very much like a community ministry, and the church felt a responsibility to progressive movements within the city.

During my time at the Community Church of Boston, my efforts to support queer, trans, and HIV-positive prisoners grew. I was eventually writing to far more prisoners than I could manage to connect with on my own, and it became clear that this needed to be shared work. One evening, I made a large dinner for friends, invited them over, and informed them that they could eat the meal I prepared after they responded to some of the letters I had from prisoners. One of my friends suggested that it was time to build a website and try to get folks beyond my friend group involved. This was when the organization Black and Pink was brought to life. I chose the name because it was going to be an explicitly anarchist and abolitionist organization, and black was the color of the flag of anarchism. Pink was the color I associated with queerness as a gay man, thanks to the use of the pink triangle as a symbol of pride by AIDS activists in the early 1990s. As such, Black and Pink was created to be a queer anarchist/abolitionist organization that would strive to meet the needs of LGBTQ/HIV-positive prisoners while organizing for the abolition of the prison industrial complex.

At the heart of Black and Pink is the pen pal program. Despite the significant power inequities between prisoners and people on the outside, there can be incredible beauty in their relationships; central to the political vision of Black and Pink is that these relationships should be mutual. Those on the outside are not simply providing charity or a service to the prisoners they are writing to—rather, these relationships are intended to be transformative for both people involved. One of the tactics of the prison industrial complex is to isolate prisoners from people on the outside and vice versa, not only with solitary confinement or building prisons far from the communities most prisoners actually come from but also in the form of mail censorship, restrictive visiting policies, and regulation of all communication between those on opposite sides of prison walls. Writing letters is one of the ways people can create cracks in the walls built to separate prisoners and people on the outside. While these letters can and should provide individual nourishment to prisoners who receive them, they also have the ability to strengthen the abolitionist movement by sharing stories of truth about a system that thrives on silence and lies.

Black and Pink was created as a secular organization, though my work within it was always a ministry for me. When I started the organization, I had not yet gone to seminary school, but my motivations and vision were shaped by my Unitarian Universalist faith. If I understood that there was no punishment after death—that there truly was no hell to fear, as John Murray claimed—and if I was to be a nontheistic humanist focused on dismantling the hells on earth, then abolishing the US prison system was a requirement of my theology. Writing letters with people and supporting others who were writing prisoners forced me to learn more about pastoral care and the need to be present with people through hard moments. I started learning the difference between listening and trying to solve problems, both of which were needed at different times. The clearest religious connection for me, though, was the deepening of my belief in the visions of abolition.

Abolition is a concept much bigger than just tearing down the concrete and steel buildings that lock people away in cages. This beautiful destruction is an essential aspect of abolition, but not necessarily where abolition begins or ends. Visions of abolition have been brilliantly offered by leading thinkers and organizers like Angela Davis, Ruth Wilson Gilmore, Mariame Kaba, and many others. While Unitarians, Universalists, and (after the two religions merged in 1961) Unitarian Universalists have engaged in prison reform efforts since the original reform of creating prisons as an alternative to corporal punishment, it was not until UU General Assembly in 2015 that we had a large group of Unitarian Universalists align with the vision of prison abolition. Many within Unitarian Universalism have focused on the specific horror of the death penalty or the overwhelming impact of the racist War on Drugs. Some have also focused on those who are presumed to be innocent. In an April 2019 article in the *New York Times*, Ruth Wilson Gilmore suggested that for abolition to be possible, people need to expand their view of who deserves empathy and attention.

"When people are looking for the relative innocence line," Gilmore told me, "in order to show how sad it is that the relatively innocent are being subjected to the forces of state-organized violence as though they were criminals, they are missing something that they could see. It isn't that hard. They could be asking whether people who have been criminalized should be subjected to the forces of organized violence. They could ask if we need organized violence."

Unitarian Universalists have a unique opportunity to connect to the abolitionist movement, a connection that is strengthened by lay and ordained community ministry. With a theology that lifts up original blessing and universal salvation, we have the capacity to understand the complexity of human behavior and the potential for healing, accountability, and transformation. It is because of our theology that I was able to remain grounded in the vision of abolition, despite the enormity of the task. With more UU community ministers engaged in abolitionist organizing and ministry, we could have far greater impact.

Black and Pink's original focus was exclusively on people who were currently incarcerated. Over time, the needs of formerly incarcerated people and court-involved people started coming up within our efforts in Boston. We slowly started to offer support to individuals with open cases by showing up at court, posting bail, and trying to help folks navigate the violence of the criminal legal system. One of the people I became closest with was a woman named Lexi.

Lexi and I first met in the kitchen of the Community Church of Boston. Six months earlier, Lexi had managed to steal all of the computers from the church office. Lexi hid in the church building after the end of the weekly meeting of BAGLY—the Boston Alliance of Gay, Lesbian, Bisexual, and Transgender Youth—and got herself into the church office. The office computers could not possibly have been worth more than one or two hundred dollars; they were many years old and had not been updated due to concerns that any new software would be the end of the dinosaurs' functioning. Regardless, Lexi's addiction to heroin and need for immediate cash filled her with the determination needed to get the computers out and sold. It was a freezing and snowy night when Lexi stole the three computers. She wrapped them up in a sheet she found in the building and, as she retells the story with a mix of pride and embarrassment, she climbed down the fire escape in high heels and hustled away into the night, computers in hand.

When the Community Church of Boston was robbed, there was an internal discussion about what to do. *Should we call the police?*

Do we file a report? At this point, I did not yet know who had stolen the computers. One of the church tenants, the American-Arab Anti-Discrimination Committee (ADC), had already been broken into and had their computer equipment stolen as well. (Lexi was not the culprit on this occasion.) The FBI was involved because of the possibility of the theft being a political attack, though many suspected that it was the FBI themselves who had stolen the ADC equipment; the Community Church of Boston had experienced years of government surveillance during the McCarthy era, at one point being called the "communist hub of New England." In more recent memory, the church had been targeted by the FBI and state police for allowing anarchist protesters to use the church as a convergence center during the 2004 Democratic National Convention. Additionally, there were active abolitionists in the congregation who had been engaged in city- and statewide work challenging the harms of the criminal legal system.

As such, the question of involving the police was both contentious and political. However, if the church didn't file some kind of report, then the insurance company wouldn't cover any of the losses. With a very limited annual budget, it would be essential to have insurance cover the cost of new computers if we had any hope of actually getting new equipment to continue the church's work.

The discussions about involving the police were primarily held by board members and office staff. The vocal abolitionists, myself included, didn't believe it was necessary to involve the police in any way; the value of the computers was so low that the insurance support would likely be insufficient to get new equipment anyhow. Rumors were already circulating about who might have stolen the computers, and fingers were primarily pointing at BAGLY.

Quickly, the question about involving the police expanded into a discussion about what it meant for a church to host LGBTQ+ young people, many of whom were youth of color, and how to create a space that would be safe for them. Involving the police wouldn't create a safe space for young people who were already disproportionately impacted by police harassment and violence. At that time, there was also no proof that someone from BAGLY had stolen the computers, and the assumptions involved in accusations were steeped in not-so-hidden racism, transphobia, homophobia, and ageism. The board and I eventually came to an agreement: we would get new computers donated to the church, and we would not file a police report.

When Lexi and I finally met in person, the congregation had moved on from concerns about the stolen computers and were at least somewhat thankful to have newer computer equipment. One of the BAGLY leaders, Trevor, asked me to meet up with him and Lexi because she had a new open case, and he was hoping that Black and Pink might be willing to provide some support to her as she went to court—her current public defender wasn't addressing her by the right name and was generally being transphobic, and Trevor hoped that Black and Pink could be a resource to Lexi as she navigated the relationship with her lawyer.

When Lexi came into the church kitchen, Trevor introduced me as the founder of Black and Pink and said that I could likely help her with her ongoing criminal cases. He then smiled and mentioned that I was the minister at the Community Church of Boston, which made Lexi leap up and run out the door. She was sure that I was there to get her in trouble for stealing the church computers, though holding Lexi accountable for stealing computers from the church wasn't a priority at that point, given the many other challenges she was navigating at that time. I was aware, though, of the complicated balance of my community ministry responsibilities to the organization I had founded and my parish ministry responsibilities to the Community Church of Boston.

Trevor and I managed to convince Lexi to come back by yelling down the stairs and sending another person after her. During our first meeting, Lexi told the story of stealing the church computers, shared her ongoing struggle with heroin addiction, and talked about turning tricks to find places to stay. It seemed that Lexi was testing me to see if I would be shocked by any of her stories, or if I would judge her and refuse to help. This was the beginning of us creating a relationship—not so much built on trust but on a mutual understanding of what we could expect from one another.

Going to court with Lexi in 2008 was one of the first times I went to court with someone for something other than a political offense. Though the courtroom was the same, the feeling was quite different. There was a greater sense of desperation. When people intentionally get arrested for a political offense, they are actively choosing to get wrapped up in the criminal legal system. The courtroom is an extension of the political action, and the feeling of righteousness permeates through the room, at least for those who are bringing a specific political agenda into the court.

A regular day in the courtroom highlights how mundane the violence of the state can be. Sitting next to Lexi on the hard benches, not dissimilar from a New England church pew, we waited and listened to the clerk call out the many names of those who came before her legal name in the alphabet. Defendants who were coming in from a jail or prison were brought in shackled around their ankles and wrists. Many were trying to hold sheets of paper in their hands and were whispering frantically with their public defenders, who were appointed to them seconds before. After brief words from the prosecution, often asking for high bail or a detainer to hold the person in jail, the defendant would be shuffled back into the holding cells to await transfer back to the jail, where they would wait for the next court date—where the same thing would happen again, until they eventually took a plea deal and would either be sentenced to more prison time or released with time served.

In my many years of going to court with people since, not once did someone ever go to trial. The daily shuffling of human beings between the police station, court, jail, prison, and back again—what guards regularly refer to as "transferring bodies"—highlights the banality of the dehumanization of criminalized people. This day in 2008 may have been one of my early times in the courtroom, but it was a process that has been going on for decades and continues today.

Courtroom support for Lexi was hardly a one-time event. Like many people struggling with homelessness, drug addiction, and mental illness, Lexi has spent the last ten years of our friendship in and out of court and jail. Over the years, Lexi had better and worse attorneys. There were attorneys who were respectful of Lexi's gender pronouns and name, and there were attorneys who were not. In certain circumstances, Lexi knew that she was going to be detained and would likely be facing jail time, and the most important thing to her was not to get the best possible outcome but to get at least some semblance of respect from the court as they sentenced her yet again.

At these times, Lexi would ask whoever was doing court support for her from Black and Pink to interrupt court proceedings by shouting out, "She goes by *Miss*," or "Her name is Lexi." Through doing court support with Lexi and, over time, other LGBTQ+ people in the Greater Boston area, Black and Pink developed a political and pastoral framework behind our court-support efforts. Most importantly, we were there to do what the person we were supporting wanted from us; our responsibility was to follow their lead. If they wanted to make a scene, we would be supportive. If they wanted to be quiet and agreeable, acquiescing to whatever was necessary to get the best possible outcome, we would be supportive. If they needed us to speak to their attorney and correct the attorney on name, pronoun, or anything related to their sexuality, we would do so. The greatest risk in the courtroom was being faced by whoever we were supporting, and our responsibility was to align with them in whatever way felt best in any given moment. The risk of being held in contempt for interrupting court was very low, and the impact it had on making someone feel seen and respected was worth the low risk. This is an important lesson for all pastoral work: accompaniment and solidarity are often the most important things ministers can offer those they are serving.

Our relationship with Lexi has not only been about showing up for her when she was facing criminal charges. When Black and Pink decided to describe ourselves as "an open family," we were committing to be there for one another in ways that extended beyond the limitations often placed on social workers or nonprofit workers. Members of Black and Pink have invited Lexi to stay in their homes, shared countless meals with her, gone with her to medical appointments, celebrated holidays with her, visited her when she was in jail, written letters while she was locked up, pushed back against her when she was acting inappropriately, shared makeup with her, and so on.

Support for Lexi has not always been about doing what she wanted. It's also been important for individuals within Black and Pink, and for Black and Pink as an organization, to establish boundaries. Setting boundaries can be really hard when someone is struggling to get their basic needs met. And yet when people in Black and Pink decided to allow Lexi to stay with them, they were encouraged to clarify expectations about sharing space. They needed to answer questions together: Could Lexi be in the house when others weren't allowed? If Lexi was using in the house, was there a place that was allowed? Was food in the kitchen up for grabs? There was also a timeline to any homestay for Lexi, a date that she needed to move on to somewhere else. While we could work on systemic change to create housing that was free and accessible to everyone, it was not within our capacity to provide permanent housing, even though it was heartbreaking to say no at times.

Lexi has always been open about her struggle with heroin addiction. When Lexi was a teenager, her mother introduced her to heroin and crack. She started actively using when she was fourteen years old and, at thirty-three, is still struggling to stop. Stopping heroin use was not a priority for Lexi until 2016. For the first eight years that she was involved with Black and Pink, Lexi sought support in managing life around her addiction, not ending her drug use. As an organization, Black and Pink has no agenda about anyone's individual drug use. There are community expectations about behavior and agreements to respect, wherever people are in their relationship to drugs and alcohol, but no expectation that an individual who uses any specific substance should be working to change their use. The blurry lines of what makes Black and Pink "an open family" can mean that individuals lean into the relationships and address what appears to be dysfunction in another's life, caused by substance use.

Over the years, I constantly navigated blurry lines in my relationship with Lexi. It was my responsibility to remind myself that my desires for Lexi's life may not have been her desires, and for me to push my agenda onto her was not only ineffective but also paternalistic and harmful to our relationship. While it was inappropriate for me to pressure her to stop using if she didn't want to, it was fair for me to create boundaries about what I could and could not provide to her. Creating my own boundaries was important for my health and the health of our relationship.

Establishing and practicing healthy boundaries is a key component of ministerial practice, whether in community or a parish. The UU Ministers Association sets important guidelines for us to practice that protect us as ministers and those we seek to serve. Healthy boundaries sustain us for a long-term ministry and help us maintain integrity when we aren't at our best; clarity in our boundaries enables those we connect with to know what to expect. In my relationship with Lexi, I also needed to be aware of my own sobriety and my family of origin's struggles with addiction, and I needed to process the feelings that came up for me with colleagues, a therapist, or my partner. Maintaining my own health was essential if I was going to fulfill my call to ministry.

In June of 2012, I stepped down from my role as minister at the Community Church of Boston. I graduated from seminary in spring 2010, and the church ordained me in the fall of that same year. I was committed to serving the congregation for two more years but knew that I wanted to dedicate more of my time to building up the work and ministry of Black and Pink. It was a giant leap of faith to leave a paying job to begin working full-time in an organization that had a budget of less than $15,000—at that point, we still had never created an annual budget. We were funding all of our work by asking friends to share money, giving many hours of time to opening mail from prisoners, and stealing copies from Kinko's to send newsletters to prisoners.

I have never connected to and continue to struggle with the language of "entrepreneurial ministry," likely in part because of my first two years full-time at Black and Pink, with no salary, and the inherent connection between entrepreneurship and individual profit. The ministry, work, and need were clear; the financial resources were not. I had to rely on other contract work, guest preaching, and assorted part-time jobs, including working at a domestic violence shelter and becoming an adjunct professor, to financially support myself while building up Black and Pink. I also let my loans go into default, ran up credit card debt, and moved in with my partner to save money (and because we were adorably in love). Michelle Alexander's book, *The New Jim Crow*, had just come out, and there wasn't yet the major increase in resources to prisoner solidarity work that was about to start coming in. Few people had ever considered the specific needs of LGBTQ+ and/or HIV-positive prisoners, so we had to be creative in our fundraising efforts.

In summer of 2012, Black and Pink became a fiscally sponsored organization by Out Now, an LGBTQ+ youth organization located in Springfield, Massachusetts. Soon after, we received our first grant for $10,000 to help us strengthen our administrative capacity and cover some of the costs of sending our newsletter of prisoner-generated content to our thousand prisoner members.

Over the next five years, we continued to grow in prisoner membership, outside volunteers, and financial resources. Chapters of Black and Pink started popping up around the country. My designation as a clergyperson increased the ease with which I was able to get into prisons to visit people, which was essential because my history of incarceration would've otherwise prohibited me from many visits. Many Unitarian Universalist churches in New England welcomed me to come and preach about abolition. Multiple churches hosted card-writing parties to prisoners during the winter holidays. In October of 2015, we had our first-ever national gathering of Black and Pink in Boston. Hundreds of people attended our celebration dinner, and fifty formerly incarcerated LGBTQ+/HIV-positive people spent the weekend together, building connections, healing, and gaining new skills. That weekend, we also released a report, *Coming Out of Concrete Closets*, based on a survey of our prisoner members. The survey results remain the largest-ever collection of data focused specifically on LGBTQ+ prisoners.

During that weekend, I also announced that I would be stepping down as the national director in summer 2017. As the white founder of an organization that primarily served people of color, it was important for me to make space for and support the leadership of Black, Indigenous, and other people of color.

The following two years were a time of massive prisoner membership growth, reaching 16,000 prisoners who received the monthly Black and Pink publication. We created new structures of leadership for the organization. We hired staff. We had many successes and challenges together. As I stepped down, we hit some big bumps, but Black and Pink is now led by an amazing executive director, Dominique Morgan, who has helped take the organization to a whole new level. One of the parallel joys of community ministry and parish ministry is learning when one needs to move on and make space for new leadership. Watching the successes and beauty of someone else coming in and learning to let go of my own agenda has been an opportunity to practice humility and unconditional love.

Community ministry does not need to fit in any boxes. As we celebrate community ministry and lift up examples of how community ministry can function, we need not prescribe a "correct" path for others to follow. Queer theology has taught us the importance of tearing down borders that restrict our beautiful selves from fulfilling our calls. Blur the lines between parish and community ministry. Blur the lines between secular and religious work. Blur the lines between professional and lay ministry. Establish clarity about what boundaries are necessary for community- and self-care, and then begin figuring out what arbitrary borders have been created that must be removed to be successful in creating a ministry that gets us closer to collective liberation. Community ministries have the capacity to give life to what will bring forth a version of the kin-dom of heaven, here and now.

Since the original writing of this essay, Lexi died of an overdose. May this story honor her life and may the memory of her inspire action that gets us closer to a day when no life is considered disposable.

Breathing New Life with BLUU

Dr. Takiyah Nur Amin

Being a Unitarian Universalist requires something of us—our shared faith calls us to sacrifice something in response to calling this place our own. What is the cost of being a Unitarian Universalist? It is the cost of working daily in our lives toward justice, equity, and compassion in human relations, of upholding a commitment to democracy without squelching the needs of marginalized voices, whose needs don't constitute a majority.

It is a willingness to care beyond ourselves for the interdependent web of which we are a part and to consider how our actions impact others at every turn. Being a Unitarian Universalist is not an easy path. If we live out this faith beyond Sunday morning, we are confronted at every turn with a chance to live out these commitments in our daily lives.

And yet, in this challenge, there is comfort. In this work toward justice-making, there is peace. We can lean into it where it may yet be found.

Rev. Takiyah Amin (she/her) is a member of the Black Lives of Unitarian Universalism Organizing Collective and a dance scholar, educator, and academic success strategist. She is the co-editor of *BLUU Notes: An Anthology of Love, Justice, and Liberation.*

One of the things that centers me in our shared faith is the work I do with Black Lives of Unitarian Universalism (BLUU) Organizing Collective. Together, we agree to be transformed in the service of the work* that we do, even when it is uncomfortable or painful. As Black UUs, we are committed to guiding each other through these seasons of transformation by offering both accountability and support. For us, this is a spiritual mandate, a calling, a commitment, indivisible from the work we do as organizers. It is this relationship between claiming our faith as UUs and using it to guide and galvanize our personal growth and efforts toward liberation that has lifted me up during some very difficult times.

I am reminded that, as Unitarian Universalists, we count Jewish and Christian teachings among the sources of our faith, which call us to respond to God's love by loving our neighbors as ourselves. As I probe those teachings about love and community, I am especially struck by the creation stories preserved in the book of Genesis in the Hebrew Bible.

Before I go further, let me say that while I am theistic in my own orientation to this faith, I recognize that words like *God* can be a challenge for some in our community, and I respect that. When I speak of God, what I mean is a power that exists beyond individual human agency—a power that arises and resides in community, as community, when we enact a shared commitment to love and equity, and to being transformed in the service of our work in making justice.

I am appealing to something beyond our individual agency, to which we yield in the building of a beloved community. That *something* is wide and deep and broad enough to hold us all across our

---

* This phrase is attributed to Mary Hooks, the former codirector of Southerners on New Ground (SONG).

differences. It looks like a community that might not be perfect for any one of us but that is good for all of us.

BLUU has become a spiritual home for many Black UUs who have been silenced, invisibilized, marginalized, or otherwise harmed in congregational life as they endeavored to live out our faith's high calling. It has also become a haven for many Black UUs who have deep relationships with existing congregations but long for culturally relevant ministry, deep theological engagement, and a space to exist free from the scrutiny of white, middle-class cultural norms. The worship opportunities and pastoral/spiritual care we offer through the BLUU Ministerial Network (BLUUMN) are sensitive to these realities; we come to our people with open hearts and consistent care for their needs as we strive to make a space where all of us, in our diverse identities as Black people, can be held.

In the book of Genesis 1:1–31, we are told that God created the world in six days. I am not here to parse the literal nature of this story or to determine what is meant by *day* or to study the historical veracity of the text. Rather, I ask that we look beyond those heady concerns to something else the narrative points to—namely, that the Spirit of Life and Love created something with speech, through words, through divine utterance. Here, we are given a glimpse into the notion that there is power in this holy breath to call something into being in a place where nothing existed before.

The authors of Genesis report that in the beginning, when God began the work of creation, a wind from God swept over the waters. In Hebrew, the word for this divine wind or spirit is *rûah*. In Genesis 2:7, this same breath is poured into and shared with humankind to bring forth life and animate our being. This same divine breath, which, we are told, hovered over the expanse of nothingness and then called the natural world into being, is breathed into God's first human creation. This breath of life is shared intimately between the human and the divine.

What comfort may we find in this narrative as we seek to do the work of dismantling white supremacy and systems of oppression that harm so many people every day? What does this old story from the wisdom literature of a minoritized people from a long time ago have to offer us now?

There is a power in us that is as close to us as our own breath, that courses through our very being. In the story from this desert community long ago, we are told that people share the divine breath that creates, that animates, that calls forth in places where there was nothing before.

BLUU's first public project was to unveil the Seven Principles of Black Lives back in autumn of 2015. The fourth principle reminds us that "experimentation and innovation must be built into our work." This willingness to embrace models that work, leave behind tools that aren't useful or relevant, and to create new possibilities—in community building, organizing, and ministry—has animated our work. This principle of experimentation and innovation has allowed us to be flexible and responsive, aspirational and creative, in living out our faith and joining with others to do the same. We reflect deeply, learn from our mistakes and our victories, and keep moving forward.

We are reminded in the first principle upheld by our member congregations that we are to affirm and promote the inherent worth and dignity of every person. Refracted through the lens of a white supremacist culture, that principle is wrongly interpreted to be about our own individual specialness, our right to perfect comfort, and a life without challenge in our congregations. Understood properly, that principle reminds us that everyone we interact with is our neighbor, one who shares that same divine breath—and that each of us is worthy of respect, a respect that includes moving through the world without being forced to navigate systems that foreclose opportunities based on race or other markers of identity.

The power that some call God, the Spirit of Life, or the healing energy that arises in community resides among us. We gather together in worship and lift up the good that comes—the God that comes—when we share in the work of dismantling oppression and enact our commitment to justice.

Too many times, I have found myself in UU congregations where the work of justice-making is separate from faith and formation. As a Black working-class woman, I find this experience confusing and alienating. My first role models for organizing, teaching, and ministry were the Black women who raised me and the community members in Buffalo, New York—many of whom were poor and Black—who showed me how to get things done. None of them would necessarily call themselves activists or organizers; they were people who were committed to the liberation of the marginalized and oppressed as a spiritual mandate, a duty to be upheld. They knew they hadn't gotten to where they were solely on their own steam or efforts and that giving back to others was a requirement for living in the world.

I wish Unitarian Universalists, with all of our theological superiority, would take a lesson from folks like the people who raised me. My grandmother would not have called it *social justice work*, but she fed those who she saw hungry. My aunt Lizzie would not have called it a *public service*, but she was committed to teaching adult learners how to read. BLUU has deepened my belief that justice-making is the evidence of our faith, worship is a posture of the heart, and that we as UUs are not, in fact, just a religion of "anything goes" or "believe whatever you want." Sure, we are not dogmatic or creedal, but we are called—each and every one of us—to find meaning and then do something with it. That "doing something" is the substance of our shared living tradition.

We have been called into being for such a time as this to live out the bonds of beloved community, to make that vision a reality. We know that no human institution is perfect, but we are reminded that we needn't be perfect to share in the work of divine creation—to use our breath, money, time, talent, resources, and collective energy to build a world where equity and justice reign. We have a chance to accept the call that life demands, that faith demands, that Unitarian Universalism demands: to embody life reaching out to life and love reaching out to love, to embody the deepest truth-telling we can find so that we might liberate ourselves and others with our stories, just as generations have found peace in the story of divine breath in the book of Genesis.

This moment asks those who benefit from the asymmetrical privileges wrought by systems of oppression to sacrifice the myth of meritocracy, to give up this notion that everything owned has been earned. Instead, this moment is calling us to examine how our social and cultural position rests on the oppression of those who have been marginalized and minoritized, erased from human narratives and left to suffer in an unjust world.

This moment asks if we will use our breath to speak truth to power, to openly challenge rhetorical violence, to make space for those who have been spoken over. BLUU has raised its voice and amplified the voices of others in this faith who have often been pushed aside or ignored, and we have done so with great personal risk. The nasty messages, innuendo, dismissals, suspicions, threats, and freighted silences that have come our way as we lift up the voices and experiences of Black UUs should be no surprise. Black liberation efforts have always been met with violent opposition, tacit dismissal, or some kind of oppression. And yet we push on because this is the work our faith demands.

We often say that "risk is real and relevant" as a way to remind ourselves of what's at stake as BLUU proceeds to live out its mission and goals. UUs everywhere can take a deep collective breath and move forward into a future that mirrors the world of equity and justice that we dream about. We can exhale our anxieties and pretensions, stop looking for the next charismatic male leader, and follow those on the front lines in the fight for love and justice—those who don't necessarily embody what we think leadership should look like or sound like or be like. As a community, we can breathe life into something new.

Breathe. May it be so. Amen, Amīn, Ashe.

Q&A with Ben Gabel

Would you tell us about the facets of your work and ministry?

I would describe my ministry as a justice-making ministry working toward dismantling systems of oppression, including white supremacy culture, ableism, and other oppressions. I do this through community organizing with those with marginalized identities.

Even though I identify as a lay community minister and I do much of my ministry with the UU Society for Community Ministries (UUSCM), my professional ministry is as a congregational administrator for the Northwest Unitarian Universalist Church in Southfield, Michigan. My experience in Unitarian Universalism includes serving as copresident of UUSCM, on the Journey Toward Wholeness Transformation Committee, on the UUA Nominating Committee, and as a past steering committee member for Diverse & Revolutionary UU Multicultural Ministries (DRUUMM). I also served on the intern minister committee for the Unitarian Universalist Ministers Association and youth adviser for the Midwest Youth Leadership School.

What informs it all is my own lived experiences as being Asian American, queer, and transracially adopted with white parents. I also grew up with two African American siblings who have significant physical and intellectual disabilities. My ministries are centered and

Ben Gabel is the former copresident of the UU Society for Community Ministries. His community ministry involves community organizing for racial, LGBTQ, and disability justice. Ben currently serves as the congregational administrator for the Northwest UU Church in Southfield, MI.

rooted in the lived experiences of a multiracial and multi-abled family. What that has brought forth for me is not only being someone who experiences different levels of marginalization but also being a witness of others who move differently in the world and witnessing those oppressions.

I think one of the pieces of the story that's interesting is that it would've been so much easier for me to do ministry through the traditional Ministerial Fellowship Committee route. However, I found that the traditional, parish-centered ministerial formation as it is in Unitarian Universalism centers the white, upper-middle-class professional's ministerial formation process. Because of my own lived experience, that process didn't make sense for me—a ministerial formation process that was counter to the ministry I am doing, both in the congregational context and in the community.

I want to challenge the notion that ministerial formation to be a UU minister is just one way, which is very limiting if we want to value dismantling white supremacy and other oppressions.

How do you think congregational and community ministry relate to each other?

Congregations are not separate from the communities in which they are located. I've done lots of community ministry in the Detroit area with the water shutdown and the pandemic. I also helped create the Metro Detroit Suburban Coalition after the death of George Floyd, a coalition mostly made up of white suburbanites understanding the racial injustices in the Metro Detroit area and recognizing the racial inequities showing up in the pandemic. That's another community ministry for me, outside of the UU context.

Our congregations still have a very paternalistic way of engaging with marginalized communities. There's a disconnect. I want to broaden the idea of Paula Cole Jones's concept of creating a "community of communities."* In order to accomplish that, we have to look at congregations as a community within a larger community.

When I came into coleadership of the UUSCM board, one of our goals was to root ourselves in relationship rather than being task- or portfolio-driven. Part of dismantling white supremacy in our organizations is to question ourselves in how we perpetuate white supremacy culture. The board was really shifting in their ways of thinking in 2019. We went with a shared copresidency model with an ordained community minister and a lay community minister to foster a model of how shared ministry could happen.

We want to elevate lay ministry as mission partners with ordained ministers. For ordained ministers, the ministerial authority comes from their educational preparation and the calling from lay folks. What we're trying to shift at UUSCM is to look at ministry, particularly community ministry, as a shared ministry between those who are ordained and called to Unitarian Universalism as an institution with lay folks who are doing community ministry in local areas.

How do you explain the difference between a lay leader and a lay community minister?

For me, a lay leader is someone who serves their faith community, such as a worship associate, maybe board president, or pastoral care

---

* Editor's note: In the 2019 Fahs Lecture, Paula Cole Jones spoke about her notion of a Community of Communities to foster inclusion and diversity. Cole Jones is the founder of A Dialogue on Race & Ethnicity (ADORE), a former president of DRUUMM, and an independent consultant specializing in multicultural competencies and institutional change. She lives in Washington, DC, and served as an interim congregational life consultant for the Central East Region from 2018 to 2020. For more on her concept of a Community of Communities, see "Creating a Community of Communities" by Paula Cole Jones and Renee Ruchotzke on UUA.org.

team. The Central East Region of the UUA has a commissioned lay minister program for those areas. Institutional ministry is those ministering to the community in which you are called to serve; that community ministry could be a prison ministry or an addiction ministry. A lay community minister is someone doing ministry with a community outside the brick-and-mortar of the UU congregation.

This is where it gets a little fuzzy between a lay leader and community ministry—for example, with social justice chairs. I was a social justice director at the Birmingham Unitarian Church. That's another piece of my puzzle.

UUSCM is a religious professional organization supporting members doing community ministry, both ordained and lay. UUSCM was founded mostly by folks who were called into UU community ministry without an ordination pathway for doing so at the time. In the early stages, it was called Society for the Larger Ministry, and it was really for folks who felt called to serve beyond our congregations. Now there is an ordination path for those folks, and the UUMA has also launched a community ministers chapter. Where UUSCM differentiates from the UUMA chapter is the belief that shared ministry is cocreated with lay community ministers, as well as lay leaders in the congregation.

How do you see the role of community ministry in our world now?

Where I see community ministry as vital lies in this question: How can we as UUs live our values to be in relationship and covenant with communities with marginalized identities? We cannot do that just within the walls of our congregations; it's impossible without forming covenant with those outside the congregations.

Take hospital chaplains as an example. They're engaging with all kinds of folks, most of whom are not UU. How do we meet the people where they are? What I get excited about is serving people.

To be blunt, I'm not interested in ministering to upper-middle-class white folks. That's the ministry that's been centered in Unitarian Universalism—we have centered ministries that serve privilege. In order to dismantle white supremacy and other oppressions, we can no longer define UU ministry as serving those who already have privilege. That's what I wrestled with in my own formation process.

It's a *both/and*. We need both the congregations *and* community ministries to live our faith in dismantling white supremacy. We often think of them as two separate ministries, but they can have that common goal. We need congregational ministers and lay leaders to know that community ministry is vital to dismantling those systems.

The Holy Work
of Administration

Rev. Dr. Lee Barker

On a sunny Sunday afternoon in May, I stood before the congregation of the First Universalist Church of Minneapolis and accepted the ministry to which I had just been ordained. I pledged myself "diligently to fulfill the offices of ministry . . . and *in all things* to live so as to show forth the way of righteousness, truth, and love among all people."

I've rarely been as weepy as I was that afternoon. This was a serious promise. My life could never be the same again. I was now obliged to serve in a way that reflected my best self and only my best self.

That day, I had yet to fully grasp that ministry is far more than the traditional folds of preacher, pastor, teacher, and activist. So much of our vocational lives are served in the demanding, behind-the-scenes work of administration. For ministers who are settled in a parish, it is the day-to-day running of the congregations. For community ministers, especially those of us who are leaders of faith-based organizations, those administrative duties comprise the largest measure of all we do.

Lee Barker (he/him) was ordained to the Unitarian Universalist ministry in 1978. Most recently he was named President Emeritus of Meadville Lombard Theological School, where he served as president from 2003 to 2019.

My own community ministry began after I had served twenty-five years in the parish ministry. When I was elected to the presidency of Meadville Lombard Theological School in Chicago, I quickly realized that my administrative skills would be integral to the school's ability to fulfill its mission. But it was the death of my father that placed me on the path of discovering that administration could be a practice that sustains me in my spiritual longings and stretch me to a deeper, more authentic engagement with the holy.

When my father died three months into my presidency, it stirred so many conflicting feelings—on the one hand, since he was elderly and suffering from dementia, I was grateful that this chapter of his life was over. On the other hand, I grieved his loss acutely. There I was, feeling so bereft as I spent my days reviewing budgets, preparing for board meetings, leading staff meetings, guiding strategic planning, making personnel decisions, developing recruitment plans, and making donor visits. I missed life in the parish, where I would have been able to name the deeper meaning of his death in the disciplined preparation and weekly sermons. I missed the pastoral encounters where I would have felt the abundance of life's healing grace. And I missed being on the front lines of community actions for peace and justice, where I would have experienced the hope that comes from direct involvement in history-making social movements. Where once my vocational life would have recentered and anchored me, I now had to admit this new position was just not doing the trick. I needed my ministry to help guide me through the deaths of those I love. I needed my work to lead me to the places of purpose and gratitude, surrender and differentiation, grace and gratitude and wonder.

I set out to discover how it could be so, and, these many years later, I can affirm unequivocally that administration can nurture the spiritual self. That's especially true in the key administrative acts of developing mission statements, undertaking strategic planning, supervising staff, and fundraising—you would be forgiven to think that these are unlikely spiritual practices. I reflect on them here as an offering to all who wish to discover the holy work of administration.

Mission, Purpose, and Gratitude

Purpose is the most powerful motivator in the world.
The secret of passion truly is purpose.
—Robin Sharma

Naturally, it is easiest to maintain a spiritual focus if one is able to identify and articulate what, for them, is life's larger purpose. For ministers, this is not such a difficult thing. If it does not come to us instinctively, it is ingrained in us by virtue of our vocational development. Time and time again, from our earliest days in seminary through the various stages of denominational credentialing and beyond, we are required to describe our personal theology and express the nature of our calling. In the most fortunate circumstances, the mission statement of the organization we serve is firmly aligned with our calling. But sometimes, it takes extra effort to make that connection explicit.

When I was elected president of the seminary in 2003, the mission of the school was pretty straightforward. Its purpose was to serve as an "educational, research, and informational center for liberal religion that prepares men and women for Unitarian Universalist ministries, advances scholarship, and empowers moral leadership in a multicultural global context." The statement made perfect sense; after all, this was a school. The purpose of every school is to educate and graduate its students, and this statement not only outlined that purpose clearly but also clarified what a school does, even beyond that core purpose. Having just completed a long stint in Unitarian

Universalist parish ministry, I had no doubt that my new position as president of this organization was well-tuned to the objectives of my life. What better way to serve my faith tradition than to assist in the formation of the next generation of religious leaders?

But I also felt that something was missing, something that anchored me to the longing of my soul.

No mission statement developed in a particular moment can be expected to endure forever. A natural time to review and update it is when a new leader comes onboard. So, early in my presidency, when the board of trustees and I determined that it was time to reconsider the mission of the school, it was important to me that any new statement specify the reason *why* we educate students and prepare them for their ministries. It took almost no persuasion for the trustees to see the rationale for that inclusion. They, too, felt like something was missing.

After an intense and comprehensive process, we arrived at the new mission statement that was not all that much different than the previous one: ". . . Our mission is to educate students in the Unitarian Universalist tradition to embody liberal religious ministry in Unitarian Universalist congregations and wherever else they are called to serve." It was a little more focused and eliminated assumptions about gender, but it still made clear that we functioned as a school. The difference came in a new, second sentence, which read, "We do this to take into the world our Unitarian Universalist vision of justice, equity, and compassion."

There! That did it! I was not leading an institution that was simply about the task of granting degrees, although that was certainly central to what we did. No, I was leading an institution that was changing the world through the efforts of the people who held our degrees. The work I was doing, along with all the others who led and taught and learned, was making the world a more just, equitable, and compassionate place. And, not surprisingly, that was the path that drew me to ministry. It was my life's purpose.

For anyone who is eager to assess the relationship between the mission of the organization they serve and their own religious values, there are several important questions to be considered. First, do you have clarity about your own theology and its underlying values? It is only possible to view an organization through the lens of your own principles and ideals if you know what those principles and ideals are.

Second, can you identify the difference between the true mission of the organization and its programs and functions? The concept of "mission creep" is based on the frequent tendency of organizations to be pulled in several directions—even if those directions are neither mission-based nor sustainable. There is often a discrepancy between what an organization should be doing and what it is doing; knowing the difference is key to understanding whether this is an organization where your own values can be served and promoted.

And finally, if you believe that there needs to be a formal review of the mission: Is the timing right for the organization to undertake what should be a comprehensive process? And can you resist the natural (and usually unwitting) temptation to bend the organization's mission to meet your own personal need for meaning? Twisting the organization's mission into what you want it to be, rather than what it should and can be, is sure to create a mismatch in your vocational life that can lead to a spiritual crisis.

But when the purpose of the organization and the values of the people who serve it are in sync with one another, the foundation has been laid for a rich spiritual life to flourish.

One of the tasks of the leader is to promote the organization to current and potential stakeholders. Once our seminary's new mission statement was in place, I would often recite it verbatim in performing that duty, and when I came to that final sentence—"We do this to take into the world our Unitarian Universalist vision of justice, equity, and compassion"—I would always well up with gratitude. After all, the fact that our community so well understood the truest, most consequential nature of our work together was genuinely gratifying. Equally so, that sentence was a personal reminder that my life's purpose could be fulfilled by my vocational life.

Planning, Surrender, and Grace

When the door is closed, you must learn
to slide across the crack of the sill.
—Yoruba proverb

Thirty-five years ago, having reaching my personal "bottom," I stopped drinking. That I have been able to keep my sobriety for as long as I have is due in part to my reliance on what is known as the Serenity Prayer. When I entered the ranks of community ministers, I could not have imagined how important that prayer would be to my work.

God grant me the serenity to accept the things I cannot change,
the courage to change the things I can, and
the wisdom to know the difference.

One of the key jobs of the leader of any faith-based organization is to point a strategic direction for the future of that organization. Like so many religious institutions, seminaries have been made vulnerable by shifting trends. The fact that fewer people, especially young adults, are affiliating religiously has meant that many traditional schools are facing a reduction in financial contributions and student enrollments. By the time I arrived in my position in 2003, an audacious plan had been adapted by the board of trustees that was intended to address these challenges. The proposal was to attract greater numbers of students by redeveloping and expanding the campus on the site it had occupied for almost seventy-five years. I was completely on board with the plan, but within several months of my arrival, it became apparent that the local neighborhood residents and institutions were adamantly opposed to the project. Without their support, it would not move forward, and so the question became: How could we otherwise expand the facility, strengthen the institution, and stay true to our mission?

Over the next seven years, we tried five different yet unsuccessful initiatives. Each, however, inched us toward our ultimate solution of relocating our campus to a twenty-first-century facility in downtown Chicago and implementing a low-residency program that required site work in multicultural institutions and churches, where students carried out classroom assignments. In this way, we met the demands of the age and erased our budget deficits.

This undertaking deepened me spiritually. As each plan failed, I had to surrender my attachment to it and, even more consequentially, surrender to circumstances that were outside of my control.

In describing *nonattachment*, the American poet Stephen Levine wrote, "It is the spaciousness to allow any quality of mind, any thought or feeling, to arise without closing around it, without eliminating the pure witness of being. It is an active receptivity to life." I came to understand that moving away from the current plan, whatever it may have been at the time, allowed for something new (and better!) to emerge if, and only if, I was able to stay open to the new possibilities—or, as I think about it now, leave open a space so wide that the grace of what is new could find its way to blossom.

The second, even more intimate way that the spiritual orientation of nonattachment and surrender brought its grace to me through these many planning processes was that in our commitment to transparency, the trustees and I were adamant about communicating the broad details of each new possibility and the rationale for considering it—despite the fact that a fresh round of controversy was discharged every time one plan was replaced by another.

There were so many false starts; I empathized with the stakeholders who became skeptical and discouraged by the process. Long before we arrived at our ultimate solution, their weariness had stormed into objections and protests. Alumni lobbied us to maintain the school by making a few tweaks here and there, ministers used their blogs to critique the school's plans, and students protested by organizing a sit-in. As president, I was the focus of much ire, and there were times when that hurt. But the future held no guarantees; I couldn't say with certainty that any of the plans would actually work. I could only assure our stakeholders that I would only commit to a final plan if our chief objectives could be met and we could better serve our students' education and achieve financial equilibrium—in short, I could support a plan only if it would allow us to bring to the world greater justice, equity, and compassion.

Along the way, I also had to consider the possibility that my actions and decisions would lead to a loss of support among the board of trustees. Even if a plan succeeded in meeting our goals, it was possible that I had become so controversial that I would have to leave my position in order for the school to move forward. I didn't want to leave, but I had to be realistic, which caused me to persistently reflect on questions about who I was in relation to my office—questions that every leader must address in difficult times, in one form or another. How much was my personal identity attached to being the president of the seminary? Was I using my presidency only to meet the needs of my ego? How embarrassed would I be if I lost my job? Would I hold back from making hard decisions for the future of the school if those decisions led to my dismissal?

In the end, I understood that I could not be the president the school needed me to be if I needed to be the president of the school. In other words, if I were going to lead the school forward, I would have to surrender my attachment to the position, its title, and my professional identity.

This was a spiritual journey and, as such, it was hard and never-ending. The results were both tangible and intangible. Ironically, when I accepted the possibility that I could lose my job, I discovered a new authority with those I sought to lead. For one thing, I wasn't invested in selling any one plan or solution, and I could identify the downside of any direction in which the school might move. (Let's face it, any innovation will have its downside, no matter how good it proves to be.) Even more so, I found that I was better inclined to access the hope of new possibilities and less inclined to concentrate on the fear of failure. I was more easily able to let go of my resentment toward my critics and summon compassion for their hurt.

I was a community minister who served as an administrator, and I had been touched by grace.

Staff Supervision, Self-Differentiation, and Compassion

> You are growing into consciousness, and my
> wish for you is that you feel no need to constrict
> yourself to make other people comfortable.
> —Ta-Nehisi Coates

As I write this, I am sitting in a coffee shop whose motto is plastered all over the walls: *If you put people first, you cannot fail.* That seems as if it could be the perfect guiding philosophy for the oversight of personnel. Every ministerial impulse suggests that if you affirm, trust, and give your staff everything they need to succeed in their jobs, you will not—you cannot—fail. Who wouldn't want to throw in their lot with an organization that so obviously recognizes the worth and value of every person? Who wouldn't want to work tirelessly and joyfully for an organization that sees the spark of divinity in every individual?

If only it were that simple. Even in a workplace that is happy and productive, the fact that it relies on human beings to function makes it an imperfect environment. Feelings get hurt, miscommunications occur, conflicts flare, budget restrictions force cutbacks, clients complain, and individual performances sag. "Putting people first" is a worthy aspiration, but it is not sufficient to perfect that which is ultimately imperfectible. A supervisor leads in the real world of tough decisions and difficult conversations, a world that calls for the spiritual quality of self-differentiation. Self-differentiation can help the supervisor make personnel decisions that enable the organization to fulfill its mission. A lack of self-awareness can undermine otherwise-achievable institutional goals.

I once interviewed an applicant for a high-level position in the school's development department where the successful candidate would work with me to identify and cultivate potential major donors. This candidate was amazing. I couldn't believe my good fortune to have discovered her—through an online ad, no less. She was a personable, accomplished, and knowledgeable professional who had an innate appreciation for the school's mission and culture. When I offered her the position, she told me there was one thing she "wasn't sure" she had mentioned: "I don't drive."

What? The job called for her to be on the road a third of her time, but she assured me that this would not interfere with her ability to travel. She went to great lengths to demonstrate how, using ride shares and public transportation, she could get to even the most remote locations to visit donors. She was insistent that this would not interfere with her performance and that she could do the job. Ignoring my doubts, I hired her.

After a few weeks of orientation, I raised the issue of travel. It was time to visit the school's strongest financial supporters so she could hear directly what motivated them to be generous. She agreed and told me that she would schedule those visits, but first she wanted to research their backgrounds so she could make her first approaches most sensitively. "Okay," I said, figuring I needed to let her do it her way. Her success would come only if she was able to draw on her own strengths.

But after a few more months, she still had not made any visits. Her reasons were many. She had to wait for the annual appeal to conclude, she tried to schedule visits but no one was going to be home, she had not yet heard back from anyone she had contacted, her husband was in an accident—all of which were plausible but, in the end, constituted a pattern that led to the obvious conclusion that I had made a hiring mistake. The fact that she did not drive was indicative of a deeper issue, one I could not specify but was somehow connected to her unwillingness to spend the time on the road that would allow her to successfully perform her job.

Meanwhile, I maintained a nagging reluctance of my own. I couldn't find it within myself to confront the problem with her. I made excuses for her, I accepted excuses from her, I promised myself I would discuss the problem at our next weekly meeting and then failed to do so. Why was I so passive? I can see it now: I was not adequately self-differentiating.

Self-differentiation is the ability to separate our own thoughts and feelings from the thoughts and feelings of others. For example, if you come home at 5:00 p.m. and find that your partner has had a miserable day and is in a foul mood, self-differentiation is the quality that keeps you from feeling responsible for their mood or feeling the need to "make them all better." You can listen to them and comfort them, but their feelings are their feelings, and your feelings are yours. Self-differentiation is not losing touch with yourself while still being able to hold a deep connection to others. It is the ingredient essential to "know thyself, and to thine own self be true."

What makes self-differentiation a fundamentally spiritual orientation is that it permits us to lead a life in which our actions are intentional and aimed at a purpose higher than the self. If we are not adequately self-differentiated, we will almost always cater to our feelings over and against our thoughts, and they alone will dictate our judgments and actions. It is not that feelings should be discounted in determining our behavior, but only a balance between intellect and emotion will serve the greatest purposes of our lives. For instance, if my life's objective is to create a more just world, the pain I hold for those who are the victims of injustice will keep me motivated, but justice will only be created by also establishing well-considered strategies to bring it into being.

The same basic principle holds true in our administrative work, especially when it comes to the supervision of personnel. Feelings will help us oversee the work of our colleagues with compassion, but they will not ever be the sole means by which problems are addressed. In the case of the struggling development professional, I honored my feelings to the exclusion of my intellect. I avoided addressing the issue because I was afraid of conflict. I ignored the problem because I wanted her to like me. I found excuses to not deal with what was happening because I internalized her thoughts and feelings.

Eventually, I was struck by two insights: First, I was not being authentically compassionate toward her because I was not treating her with dignity, respect, or fairness. How could I convince myself that I was regarding the fullness of her humanity if I was unwilling to be vulnerable with her by fully and directly voicing the truth of my disappointment? How could I say that I believed in the potential of people to grow and change if I was unwilling to help her overcome shortfalls in her performance?

Second, by ignoring the problem, I was not fulfilling my own life's purpose. If my commitment was to bring greater justice, equity, and compassion to the world, and the means by which I did that was by leading this school, then the institution needed to be as strong as it possibly could be. And that meant it needed a robust development effort with successful and supported development staff.

The way became clear. I would have to take the more compassionate route of giving difficult, direct feedback and guidance. I would have to boost my ability to be better self-differentiated.

My community ministry in administration had issued an invitation to spiritual growth. I knew I had to accept.

Fundraising, Intimacy, and the Holy

Success isn't about how much money you make,
it's about the difference you make in people's lives.
—Michelle Obama

It may be that there is no administrative duty more in need of self-differentiation than that of asking people face-to-face for their financial support. Most people have a hard time asking other people for money, even for the worthiest causes.

But not only is that the responsibility of all community ministers who oversee not-for-profit organizations but it is a duty that occurs in an increasingly competitive environment in which there has been a proliferation of such organizations. From 2005 to 2015, the number of charitable organizations registered with the IRS rose from 1.41 million to 1.56 million, an increase of 10.4 percent. This is even more challenging in the world of religion, where the decline in the number of people who are institutionally affiliated means, obviously, that there are fewer prospective donors to draw upon. In today's big politics, there may be a fundraising bias toward soliciting a large number of small donations, but in the places where community ministry is carried out, there is a need to rely on donors who make larger gifts. That is not to discount the importance of financial support at all levels, but it is almost always the support of major donors that guarantees the vibrant and effective fulfillment of a mission.

All of which is to say that, as community ministers, we will find ourselves in the living rooms of people, asking for their financial support.

We think of money as a personal matter, and initiating a discussion about it has the potential to arouse any number of emotional responses, from fear and shame to pride and contentment, from anxiety and helplessness to safety and security, from envy and intimidation to gratitude and superiority. Our relationship to money is a central component of our identity, so it is no wonder that even the most experienced administrators have a hard time moving beyond their emotions when it comes time to ask a potential donor to make a major financial gift.

Clergy are often especially uncomfortable with "making asks." It is in our nature to focus on a person's spiritual life, and we correctly assume that their wealth is completely unrelated to the depth of their soul. To engage with a person because they have wealth, and because we hope they will be willing to share a portion of that wealth with our organization, has the potential to reduce the relationship to something that is merely transactional and profane. But I have found just the opposite to be true. These asks of individuals were among the peak experiences of my seminary presidency—and that had nothing to do with whether the ask resulted in a gift.

Early in my ministry, my fundraising "technique" with major donors was to make soft asks. I would visit a potential donor in their home, listen to their dreams for the school and articulate my vision for it, and then I would silently pray that they would raise the topic of money. Sometimes my prayers would be answered, and the prospective donor would initiate the possibility of making a gift. What a relief! On those occasions, I would gratefully offer them some opportunities for how they could support the school. Other times, the topic never came up and I moved on to my next appointment. I can only imagine how some people scratched their heads over the reason for my visit. They understood my role as president; they knew that an element of my position was to engage potential funders and ask them for their support and they invited me into their homes to give me a chance to do that, but I did not rise to the occasion.

I didn't become comfortable making donor visits until I asked myself, "Why is it that, as a minister, I can initiate conversations with people about matters as personal as their broken relationships and their impending deaths, but I can't bring up the subject of money?" In that question, I found my answer: Conversations about money require the same degree of intimacy and trust as any pastoral conversation, and, like any pastoral encounter, a conversation about money calls for a deep examination of values and principles. For me, intimacy, trust, and the explication of values are the three ingredients that make pastoral visits holy encounters—the elements that make donor visits far more pastoral than mercenary.

As we make our request for financial support, we listen intently to the dreams and values of that person, we hear the most confidential details about their life circumstances, we offer them a way to bring to life their dreams, and we bear witness to great acts of generosity and gratitude. With that understanding, I gained the confidence to make direct appeals for financial support. In those circles of trust and intimacy, I was again and again seized by awe and wonder and gratitude.

Many times, what began as a request for support for the school often grew into personal, loving, and transformative relationships where we have been present for one another in all the times of our lives. Not too long ago, one such person—now elderly and suffering from chronic illness—told me that when the time came, she would like me to speak at her memorial service. "After all," she said, "you know me as well, if not better, than anyone else."

I was humbled by the request and could not help but remember the first time we met, in the lunchroom in the offices where she worked. I asked her if she would make a gift to the school. Over the course of our conversation, I heard about her two sons, one now deceased and the other severely disabled. She recalled the day they were born and how she had great hopes for the world that they would inherit. And then she said yes. She wanted to support the school because she still believed in that world and could see that the school was helping it come to be.

It was a moment for holiness. Yet again, I was gripped by awe and wonder and gratitude.

Spiritual Growth

Each activity of daily life in which we stretch
ourselves on behalf of others is a prayer of action.
—Richard J. Foster

When the president of a seminary is newly elected, they are invited by the accrediting body, the Association of Theological Schools, to attend a seminar for new presidents. At that gathering in my first year, the chief executive officer of the association had advice for us that stayed with me throughout the sixteen years of my presidency: "Now that you are president, your lives will be so full of administrative tasks that you will find that your goal is no longer to write that next book. Your goal will be to read that next book." He then went on to say, "You will come across people who will try to convince you that you have now abandoned the intellectual life. Don't believe it. This is the hardest intellectual work you will ever do."

He was right. The life of administration is the life of problem-solving at a level and degree of complexity that few ever have the privilege to know.

I can offer a twist on his observation by saying this: As community ministers who are absorbed in the life of administration, you will come across people who will try to convince you that you have abandoned the spiritual life. Don't believe it. This is the hardest spiritual work you will ever do.

As one who taught administration to ministerial students for more than a dozen years, I had but one aim—to open their eyes to the fact that administration is not a diversion from ministry. Administration *is* ministry, and ministerial administration does not require one to relinquish the spiritual life. Indeed, administration is a path for spiritual growth that is both demanding and rewarding.

For community ministers who have been called to the life of administration, I offer this simple concluding prayer:

Spirit of Life,
These ministers have been called to daunting and unrelenting work. May they be ever sustained by it:
witnessing the gift of grace that emerges in strategic planning meetings,

offering the balm of compassion necessary to complete the annual staff evaluation process,

unleashing deep purpose and commitment in the conception of a mission statement.

May they always know their work is holy work, bringing to life the dreams of their hopes.

Amen.

How to End the Rally

Rev. Elizabeth Nguyen

1.

It's the night before a rally in support of Saray, a Cambodian man, father, and member of the Lawrence, Massachusetts, community for decades. He has been told he must check in with Immigration and Customs Enforcement. When he goes, he faces the possibility of being detained by ICE and deported to Cambodia. Local organizing groups, his family, and his legal team are gathering to show up in solidarity as he checks in. His daughter is home from college in case this is the last time she sees her father. My friend and organizer, Kevin Lam with the Asian American Resource Workshop, one of the organizations supporting Saray, texts me: "I don't know how we should end the rally tomorrow . . . I don't know what the space should be like as we wait to see if Saray is detained or allowed to walk out free. Could you do something at the end?" Kevin is asking me to do what some people call ministry—help us be together through this impossible moment.

Rev. Elizabeth Nguyen (she/her) currently works at the intersections of immigration, incarceration, and freedom. Her community ministry has also taken the form of faith-based justice work, youth organizing, supporting progressive movement in the Vietnamese American community, and feeding people.

2.

Trayvon Martin had been murdered by police. And Michael Brown had been murdered by police. And many others. And communities across the country took our heartbreak and rage and grief and fear for our loved ones to town halls and police precincts and corner stores and into the streets. In Boston, Massachusetts, I was a few years out of seminary, ordained as a minister and serving as a director of programs at Boston Mobilization, a grassroots social justice youth organization. I learned and facilitated and organized alongside young people as we taught each other about systems of oppression, healing, and freedom. We organized around campaigns to raise the minimum wage, increase the state budget for youth jobs, and add social workers to high schools. We ate a lot of popcorn, caused a lot of ruckus, made mistakes, and grew. The young people I had the honor of being with as they facilitated workshops in their schools and for their fellow youth interns understood the necessity and power of disruptive protest, and they knew their lives and humanity were also on the line as young Black, Latine, Asian, and Arab young people—and as young white people.

Many nights during the summer of 2014, which became fall and winter, groups would call for protests and young people would show up at our scrappy office space in the Democracy Center in Harvard Square. We would make signs, stuff snacks in our pockets, and we adult staff would harangue youth into calling their parents to make sure they had some semblance of permission and conversation before we would hop on the Red Line to join the waves of people chanting "Black Lives Matter" and Assata Shakur's words, "It is our duty to fight for our freedom. It is our duty to win. We must love each other and support each other. We have nothing to lose but our chains," and, "We're young, we're strong, and we're marching all night long." There was power and clarity and integrity, and it was intense. Groups would move to block entrances to the MBTA, hold busy streets and halt traffic, or try to storm onto I-93, the shadow of the Suffolk County jail looking down at us, a constant reminder of who is punished for what in this country, of the walls that persist in dividing us even when we are only feet away from each other.

My role was to support, to be alongside. The young people were going to go into the streets whether or not we were with them, and they were young and strong and intent on marching all night long. There we were, together, dashing into the Prudential Center to pee; the young people getting on the megaphone to lead chants, tell stories, and make demands; me begging them to update their parents now and then; all of us handing out snacks, water, and cough drops and sharing a beat or word about freedom or love or survival, despite it all. I would try to stay until the last one went home. By then, the more respectable, well-known clergy were often long gone, folks with day jobs, too, and children at home, and it would mostly be young Black and brown folks, alive with vision and sometimes made sharp by suffering and the injustice of it all. There were all the things that happen when truth bursts through and the political weather is right and something becomes possible that once was not: white anarchists trying to take the mic, impromptu drum and dance circles amidst cop cars, all the types of police—bike, motorcycle, SWAT, undercover cops in Bruins gear hauled in from outside the city, looking terrified and deadly with the names of their respective Boston suburbs plastered across their chests. And there were all the other things, too—people moving in their dignity, reclaiming voice and space, sharing resources across boundaries upheld by centuries of violence, and teaching me to go where your people are. You minister to the ones you serve, and you can't minister to them if you're not there.

The nights blur together, but the feeling was the same: *Our freedoms are each other's. As long as you are in these streets, I am. As long as you are fighting for life, I am.*

3.

Inside an ICE prison, folks are organizing, advocating for each other, sharing legal advice and spiritual wisdom about surviving incarceration, and pooling money and support for those who have none. Outside the walls, faith folks and many others are catalyzed by the 2016 presidential election into action. We're having a gathering. We don't have a name or way to receive donations or a website. We have practices. We go to court with folks. We answer phone calls from ICE jail. We try to find lawyers. We raise money for immigration bond or legal needs or rent. As the shape of this network has emerged, so have its values—but they are values in practice, not articulated anywhere besides in our actions and relationships. I have a call with a trusted colleague and dear friend, Helen Bennet, who has advised and led many Jewish social justice communities and their leaders. I don't even plan to bring up the values, but as we're catching up and chatting it through, I do. She encourages me to write them down, to bring them to the gathering. I shoot off a draft to some of our key team in moments.

+ We honor people's dignity and choices in a system that denies dignity and choice.
+ We expect messiness, confusion, and discomfort, and we also choose courage and trust.
+ We judge the system, not people.
+ We fight for one another as family because we are.

People give some feedback, and we share the values at our gathering. There's some refining, and before long, people are using them as prompts for reflection on phone calls, writing them on chart paper in faith communities all over Boston to explain what we do, and adding them to email signatures, Facebook pages, our eventual website. The values are unabashedly theological, provocative, and useful; they give language to complex things in a simple way. I didn't really come up with them—rather, I saw that they reflected how we were being, and I reflected that back to us. We shared the values with friends and comrades who also were creating accompaniment networks and immigration bond funds. People took words, ideas, energy, and ethos from them and ran with it, incorporating pieces into their own work and leaving what they didn't need. It's one of the most religious things I can think of, to articulate and commit to a set of values that we will always fall short of, that we will always be practicing, and then to live them, calling each other back to them, letting us be changed by our commitments. To minister by reflecting back again and again that this is what we are doing and how.

What Is Community Ministry?

For me, community ministry is a way of explaining that there are those of us who are accountable to and ministering with people who are not in the formal structure of what is recognized as a Unitarian Universalist congregation. Some of the places that I first come to see as community ministry are the Unitarian Universalist Community Cooperatives. In 2019, UUCC is two housing cooperatives in Roxbury, Massachusetts, and when we begin them, we speak often about how diverse Unitarian Universalism is theologically, and how not-diverse it is in terms of structures or institutions. Many faith traditions have houses of worship, yes, but also schools, cafes, centers for healing in body or in spirit, nonprofits of many stripes, and more. Community ministers are as diverse as the communities or structures we serve in, and *how* we serve and *who* we serve matters as profoundly for community ministers as it does for congregational ones.

As a multiracial person with the privilege to sometimes pass as white, as a person raised with financial resources and educational access, as a citizen and a person who is currently able-bodied and cisgender, it's part of my faithfulness to unequivocally, with humility and the help of god, be on the side of those most impacted by the violence of systems of oppression. That has meant choosing ministry where I am serving the people who I strive to be accountable to, in community with, and alongside in the struggle for freedom and justice—where my Unitarian Universalism and belief that no one is very outside of the circle of love and that we all have inherent worth and dignity can be made real by action. Ministering with the people I cast my lot with for justice for all is core to my ministry, wherever I serve—in a congregation or a community setting.

Many ministers who serve in traditional congregational settings have found ways to similarly serve the people, while some community ministers do not necessarily center the work of justice or serve people who are not white and wealthy. In the streets in 2014, and in many streets before that and since, we chant, "Who do you protect? Who do you serve?" in response to police violence. As Unitarian Universalist community ministers, whether we are chaplains, practitioners in private practice, or serving faith-based institutions or other nonprofits, we must reckon with the same questions: Who do we protect? Who do we serve? Whose spiritual well-being do we tend to? Whose healing do we fight for? Who is asking us for ministry but not being served by us because there is not a formal role and funding for it? Whose milestones do we mourn and celebrate? Whose culture of prayer and song and sympathy and care do we practice?

There is a song by Shoshana Jedwab, based on the book of Ruth, that is sung by many in our faith in these times.

"Where You Go, I Will Go Beloved"

Where you go, I will go Beloved,
Where you go, I will go
'Cause your people are my people
Your divine, my divine

Maria, who is in sanctuary at a congregation, and my colleague, Rev. Annie Gonzalez Milliken, wrote a Spanish translation.

Donde vayas, yo voy querida,
Donde vayas, yo voy
Porque tu pueblo es mi pueblo
Tu pueblo es mío
Tu dios también mío.

I've sung it in organizing meetings and to myself as a prayer, amongst Unitarian Universalists of color and dear friends getting out of ICE prison who have never heard the words *Unitarian Universalist* before. For me, ministry is about serving my understanding of god, unapologetic about my theology but loosed from a need for people to understand my work as community ministry or Unitarian Universalist ministry. I am clear and proud about both of those things; they ground me personally in profound ways. And still more essential to me, in this chapter of my life and ministry, is what I do and how I do it and who I serve.

Where you go, I will go. Your people are my people, and my people are yours.

We first hear Saray's daughter speak when he checks in at the ICE office. She talks about how she wants people to know that it was his support that got her to college, about the impact on her family of not knowing if he will walk out of that office that day. She tells us all, "You can take my father, but you can't break my family."

And I tell my colleague, Kevin, that yes, I will find a thing to say, a way to hold the impossible thing of not knowing if Saray will come out free or be deported. It remains one of the most tender, sacred moments of my ministry—to be asked by a fellow queer, progressive Vietnamese organizer to offer some container for the most painful situation. To be told, without these words, *We are asking you to be our minister, and we trust you to offer a way through for a group of people with no religion in common, some of whom have been hurt by religion and some of whom are deeply religious, most of whom have never met you.*

I have us take deep breaths and feel the earth beneath us. I remind us that, as Southeast Asians, we are connected to many lands that nourish and ground us, even through violence. I call on our resilience as people who have survived refugee camps and war, displacement and resettlement, detention and deportation. And then I lead us in a call-and-response.

I say, "We are."

And everyone answers back, "Family."

We are family. Whether we have benefited from this current immigration system or are being harmed by it. Whether we have a criminal charge or not. Whether we are Cambodian, Vietnamese, Honduran, Nicaraguan, Ugandan, Indigenous to North America. Whether we are heartbroken or hopeful. We are. Family.

Many people are asking for ritual, nourishment, song, values, presence, and accompaniment alongside. In the midst of shifting denominations, cultures, structures, credentialing, and our own lives and preferences, may we find a way to minister for the people we are called to serve and who are calling us to serve. For justice, for family.

Editor's note: Not long after this chapter was finalized, the insurrection at the US Capitol happened on January 6, 2021. Rev. Elizabeth Nguyen posted a poetic prayer on Facebook that was shared widely and used in worship services that following Sunday. Rev. Nguyen gave us permission to include it here. It is a clear example of her prophetic community ministry.

Prayer for Protection

For Black, Indigenous, Muslim, Latina elected officials
for the residents of Washington, DC
For each of us who has ever been handcuffed or teargassed or afraid
     of police or white supremacists or our government
For each of us who is afraid every day for ourselves or our loved ones
     or our children or this country.
May we be protected.
May we be protected from generations of violence and hate,
from pandemic and sickness and fear.
May we be protected not because we have earned it but because of
     the generous grace of justice and spirit.
And may those of us who can be protectors, protect.
Be pourers of tea for ourselves and others, builders of power for love
     for ourselves and others,
reminders to breathe and eat and fight and tend, to rest and risk so
     we may all be protected.
And in our doubt and stress, may we rest in the air and the earth and
     the sky that have seen governments come and go, despots and
     haters come and go, that hold our bones and our breath with
     sacredness and survival.

Q&A with
Julica Hermann de la Fuente

Would you describe your experience with community ministry?

I was the first of the coordinators of the Beloved Conversations program, when Beloved Conversations got so big that Mark Hicks needed help administering it. I would talk about it to ministers and churches and coordinate with retreat leaders. I'm also a retreat leader and, most recently, part of the curriculum team, converting it to virtual.

In entrepreneurial community ministry, I do antiracism coaching for religious professionals—mostly ministers—and hang out my shingle, make myself available. Then I did it through the Unitarian Universalists Minister Association (UUMA). When I was the UUMA intern, I started institutionalizing my work, and now it's part of my work at Minneapolis. The clients pay the church, so I'm bringing in funds, but it's nowhere near what the church pays me.

Before ministry, I was a life coach and a diversity facilitator and trainer. It's like I found the people that I wanted to do the work with, within the work I was already doing.

Julica Hermann de la Fuente (she/ella) provides antiracism coaching and consulting to religious professionals and lay leaders across the US. She is also currently completing her path toward ordination. This interview was conducted while she was serving as the Director of Liberation and Transformation Ministries at the First Universalist Church of Minneapolis.

What's important about this niche is that it's a faith community. A secular conversation around diversity does not have the depth of a spiritual one. For us, antiracism is faith formation when we do it well, and that makes all the difference.

Would you share about your path to ministry?

I was called to ministry earlier in my life, before I became a life coach, but I postponed that call. I experienced a clouds-parting, angels-singing experience at the ordination of one of my friends. When I went to her ordination, during the laying-on of hands, I thought to myself, *This should be me.* Back then, I was in grad school at University of Michigan, and I couldn't take one more book. I had a role model who went to seminary in my fifties, so I thought I would go to seminary as a second career. In my early forties, I decided to go to seminary.

When things were especially hard and I was losing my patience with supporting affluent white women in finding their happiness as a life coach. When I was in grad school, I did a lot of antiracism work. I wanted to return to that. There was this little voice that said, *How about this ministry? Do we really have to wait until our fifties?*

You're now the director of Liberation and Transformation Ministries for First Universalist Church of Minneapolis. Do you still consider yourself a community minister?

I think I am a parish minister who needs to reorganize her role to have a little more clarity; I would like it to be that of an affiliated community minister. The way I want my ministry to be and the way I think is most powerful is as a trainer, a coach. I see myself moving away from the parish. I'm fortunate to be in a large system at

First Universalist, a large congregation, that wants me to play to my strengths.

Parish creates structure and containers. It's hard, but it's clearer. Community ministry can be so varied. It's helpful for you to know what your lane is and what your strengths are and play to those. I really appreciate Pamela Slim's book, *Body of Work: Finding the Thread That Ties Your Story Together*, where she discusses the idea that we all have a body of work or, in our words, a call. It's our job not only to find what we're supposed to do but also the best place to do it, where I can be me and still valuable and needed in the world. It requires a certain level of self-differentiation. That's not so much advice as a prayer. May you stay strong, and may there be flexibility in your call when it changes.

Is there anything else you'd like to share for those considering a call outside the parish?

Community ministry is part of the way that we are pushing against white supremacy cultures in Unitarian Universalism. We don't exactly fit, it's not easy to name, and that is good. That is part of the work we need to do. If you don't feel like you fit and it's not easy to find where you belong, that might be a sign that you're part of the project of liberation. Have courage. Stay with it. Find your community ministry and bring it.

Accountability to the People, Water, and Web of Life

Aly Tharp

In fall of 2012, I was twenty-two years old and had just graduated from an undergraduate environmental studies program in north Texas. My number-one priority at the time was packing as much adventure as possible into the six-month window before the student loan agencies started calling.

I was like a seed drifting in the wind, living freely and not planning on heading back to Texas anytime soon. But the adventures of that year were more intense and closer to home than I could have ever imagined.

For years, almost every national environmental organization in the US had been putting their weight behind trying to stop Trans-Canada (now TC Energy)'s proposed Keystone XL pipeline, to stem the flow of Canadian tar sands oil from crossing the Ogallala Aquifer, the Great Plains, and the piney woods of east Texas, all the way to the Texas Gulf coast for refining, selling, and ultimately burning into energy and pollution.

Aly Tharp (she/they) is a lay community minister with the UU Society of Community Ministries and a senior organizer with GreenFaith. This chapter was written while she was serving as codirector of programs and partnerships for the Unitarian Universalist Ministry for Earth (UUMFE). Her ministry is rooted in using arts and community organizing to advance climate justice..

Then-President Barack Obama permitted the construction of the last section of the project going from Cushing, Oklahoma, to the Texas coast by executive order in March 2012. I assume he did this because he was vying for favor on both sides of the issue during his reelection year.

Per usual, the news media hardly mentioned it. But the national environmental organizations were pretty quiet about it, too, and as a result, I had no idea that the portion of the pipeline running through Texas—two hours from where I was raised in the Dallas–Fort Worth metroplex—had been approved.

I found out about "KXL South," aka the Gulf Coast Pipeline, from headlines about the on-the-ground and in-the-trees resistance. A landowner in Winnsboro, Texas, who had spent years trying to prevent the pipeline from running through his family's property and had it taken by eminent domain, decided to resist the construction by building a tree-sit.

David Daniel, the landowner, was supported by a handful of students from the University of North Texas and committed land-defense activists who opposed the pipeline. Together they rigged a complex of platforms that could hold up to fourteen people, stretching across the entire two-hundred-and-fifty-meter easement for the pipeline.

Hanging from a large barricade wall was a fifty-foot banner with a large open palm on it, reading YOU SHALL NOT PASS, the famous line that Gandalf the Grey says to the Balrog demon in *The Lord of the Rings*. The blockade soon became known as Middle Earth, again in reference to *The Lord of the Rings* universe.

To protect and sustain the tree-sit, activists locked themselves to machines and blockaded the destruction of the forest as the machines and work crews inched their way south toward David Daniels' property. As I combed through the news coverage, I saw multiple

Unitarian Universalists wearing "Side with Love"T-shirts among the photos of those risking arrest. One of the UUs was Benjamin Franklin Sequoyah Craft-Rendon from Houston. Ben was locked to a feller buncher—a machine that can cut down a tree in mere seconds—with one other person, using what is called a lockbox. My blood boiled as I read Ben's testimony about what happened during their arrest.

The TransCanada site manager was very involved in encouraging the sheriffs as they used pain compliance to force Ben and the other protester to unlock themselves, handcuffing their free arms in stress positions, pepper spraying into the lockbox tube onto their skin (against federal chemical safety codes), and tasering them.

I was livid. I searched through the blogs and news articles to find out how I could support these UUs and other activists who were putting themselves directly in the way of the pipeline—known as the Tar Sands Blockade—and I resolved, in that instant, to head home and join them.

For me, this was equivalent to jumping into the deep end of the pool without knowing how to swim. I grew up in a quiet, corporate suburb, completely sheltered from exposure to popular struggles or the pollution of the corporations headquartered nearby. I only knew about environmental justice on a vague intellectual level.

Working directly with people who live in the path of the tar sands pipelines—and in the communities in Houston, where people are constantly inundated with chemicals in their air and water, trying to secure a chance to breathe —completely changed me. My understanding and support for environmental justice went from being abstract to something deeper, more accountable, and more heart-centered.

This is one of the great powers of community ministry: creating transformative relationships that bridge common divides of identity, power, and privilege, awakening community consciousness and connectedness. Being an activist, community organizer, or community minister for the long haul requires a willingness to be transformed by the work you do. To paraphrase the mother of Afrofuturism, Octavia E. Butler, we change when we shape change. I and many others involved were transformed by the Tar Sands Blockade campaign, and the campaign was transformed by each of us.

There is a small, Wendell Berry–loving Baptist church in east Texas called the Austin Heights Baptist Church. Austin Heights is not your typical Baptist church, perhaps evidenced most by the fact that they welcomed the Tar Sands Blockade into their church and into their homes. The church had been praying for a vibrant young adult program, and there we were, a bunch of stinky young adults in need of showers and a community support system—an unlikely answer to their prayers.

Austin Heights opened their property to us for strategy retreats and public events. Members of Austin Heights invited us to a potluck after church every single Sunday, helped us find a property to stay on, brought us firewood, helped us dig gardens and composting toilets, and helped us take showers and wash our clothes. They invited us to their holiday parties. We became family and continue to be family to this day.

With sustained direct-action campaigns where you're taking big risks and going against the common grain, community support can literally be a lifeline. I often wonder how differently the campaign would have gone if it wasn't for the transformative love and support that Austin Heights Baptist Church offered to us. More than anything else, the church's revolutionary power to support activist communities is what fuels my passion for my work for climate justice with Unitarian Universalists.

The closest Unitarian Universalist parallel to the ministry of Austin Heights Baptist Church that I have witnessed in recent years is the engagement of the Unitarian Universalist Fellowship and Church of Bismarck-Mandan, North Dakota, in supporting the Oceti Sakowin Camp at Standing Rock, in prayerful protection of water from the Dakota Access Pipeline (DAPL). This fellowship was the *only* faith community in the entire Bismarck-Mandan area to actively support and join the Water Protectors at Standing Rock. They did so by working in the kitchen, providing rides, raising funds, building a yurt to host travelers, inviting water protectors to speak at church worship services, and respecting the leadership of the camp elders. The congregation also worked with the Side with Love campaign to support the arrival of hundreds of Unitarian Universalists and faith leaders from many traditions who came to Oceti Sakowin Camp from across Turtle Island.

Similarly, this engagement was deeply transformative and revolutionary for all involved. The relationships and partnerships formed throughout this time continue to create ripple effects in justice movements and Unitarian Universalist ministries, helping to inspire and prepare us for the work that lies ahead.

For example, Rev. Karen Van Fossan was the part-time (and then full-time) minister of the Unitarian Universalist Fellowship and Church of Bismarck-Mandan throughout the Oceti Sakowin Water Protector uprising. She supported her congregation and the entire Unitarian Universalist faith in deepening partnership and prophetic witness of solidarity with Indigenous Water Protectors. Rev. Karen Van Fossan is now a community minister with the UUA Green Sanctuary program and supports a network of congregations and Unitarian Universalist activists to engage in a ministry of mutual support with five Indigenous Water Protectors who have spent years as political prisoners of the Dakota Access Pipeline struggle. The spark of the Oceti Sakowin Water Protector uprising lit a fire for ongoing community ministries that are transforming the spirit and practice of Unitarian Universalism in subtle and profound ways.

Climate change is projected to profoundly impact our whole planet, especially if we don't take immediate actions to address the problem—and those who contributed the least to the climate crisis are among the first and worst impacted. This is a fundamental injustice of climate change.

The Unitarian Universalist Association acknowledges climate change as a justice issue and asserts that we have a moral obligation to do what we can to prevent it from getting catastrophic. In 2006, the UUA General Assembly passed a statement of conscience about global warming, which states,

> Unitarian Universalists are called to defer to a balance between our individual needs and those of all other organisms. Entire cultures, nations, and life forms are at risk of extinction while basic human rights to adequate supplies of food, fresh water, and health as well as sustainable livelihoods for humans are being undermined.

Extinction. That's what we are risking, for far too many lives and precious things.

The twenty-first century will be defined by how we respond to climate change and ecological unraveling. To survive and to live out our Unitarian Universalist values in this life-threatened time requires transitioning from an extractive, exploitative, and unsustainable way of life to a life-sustaining society driven toward social and ecological well-being through courage, cooperation, and regeneration of Earth's abundance. Anything less and the Principles of Unitarian Universalism will ring profoundly hollow to our future generations.

Unitarian Universalist Ministry for Earth's mission is to be a wellspring of spiritual and educational grounding and practical support for bold, accountable action for environmental justice, climate justice, and the flourishing of all life. As UUMFE's codirector of programs and partnerships, I am blessed with witnessing and supporting this mission daily. The Unitarian Universalist faith has an important role to play in this transition, and there are literally hundreds of UU churches and community ministries currently engaging with this issue. I have met environmental justice community leaders who are UU, leading-edge pollution scientists who are UU, solar entrepreneurs who are UU, youth climate-strike leaders who are UU—the list goes on. I love working with and supporting these leaders and communities, and I love imagining all of the life-transforming beauty that will emerge through this essential calling of protecting and restoring the ecological and social well-being in the years and decades to come.

Slowly, surely, we are learning what it means to be accountable to one another, the water, and the Web of Life.

Bivocational Ministry

Rev. Christian Schmidt

The first time someone cried during a call about their taxes, I was surprised, but I knew what to do. Years of pastoral experience dealing with people in crisis taught me to recognize someone who needed two things: a supportive listener, and to know that they weren't alone. The crying stopped after a few moments and the story came out. A difficult family situation, a lifelong phobia of math, and continually building anxiety had made taxes into something this client couldn't even think about without freaking out.

In this case, unlike too many times in ministry, I could do something specific and helpful: I could help this person sort out a complicated tax situation and make a monthly payment plan they could afford with the IRS.

I never suspected my tax clients would need so much pastoral care, or that all the things I've learned running a small business would help so much in parish ministry.

For the last seven years, I have served different congregations as a parish minister. And for the last three years, I've also been a tax preparer. I serve half-time as senior co-minister of the Unitarian

Rev. Christian Schmidt (he/him) has served in both congregational and community ministry for most of his ministerial career, including as a parish minister, tax preparer, and consultant. His community ministry serves his colleagues in ministry by demystifying clergy taxes.

Universalist Church of Berkeley (UUCB), I run a seasonal small business preparing tax returns for clergy and their families, and I consult with congregations that are searching for ministers.

In other words, I am bivocational (and sometimes trivocational!), working multiple jobs, both religious and secular. I have also worked in both paid and volunteer positions for religious nonprofit groups over the years. And my wife, the Rev. Kristin Grassel Schmidt—who is also my co-minister at UUCB—and I have four kids we're raising, ages five to nine.

If you had asked me twelve years ago if I expected to be here, I would have been as shocked as anyone. At that time, I had an inkling that ministry might be in my future, but nothing quite like this.

When I entered seminary in 2009, I fully intended to do parish ministry. My work in the parish has been both everything I could have imagined and so much more. Meeting Kristin, who was almost done with her ministerial formation as I was starting mine, was a wonderful surprise. Thinking about and then embarking on co-ministry—that is, a shared ministry with two ministers in equal roles, often, though not always, a couple—has been a rewarding, challenging, transformational journey.

It's also come with challenges, perhaps the foremost being that working together as a co-ministry team meant that most of the positions we looked at were congregations seeking one minister, so we would be splitting one full-time job. Both of us have worked in other positions—sometimes in other congregations—to supplement our family's income.

Like many couples in their thirties, we didn't have a lot of money, and we *did* have quite a lot of student debt, which starting ministerial salaries weren't making a huge dent into. Thinking creatively about how our family could make an income was a necessity. Both of us sought out various opportunities. Kristin worked for a bed-and-breakfast (she hated the hours, other staff, and more than a few of the guests); I was the only staff member for a small UU organization. She's listed on The Knot as a wedding officiant, and I've done two temporary, part-time parish ministries.

It was a few years into our ministries that I had a strange idea: getting into the tax preparation business. I had been frustrated with trying to do my own taxes (clergy taxes are complicated and weird) and equally frustrated with trying to find a qualified tax professional to do them for me. And I thought, *Surely I can't be the only minister having this problem, right?*

Clergy taxes are so strange. First, clergy aren't technically employees of their church but rather independent contractors who have agreed to provide services. This affects so-called payroll taxes, which support Social Security and Medicare—ministers pay for this all themselves, whereas most employers pay half of those for employees. With that said, ministers also get the benefit of deducting their housing costs from their taxable income, which dates back all the way to colonial days (and again in the Internal Revenue Code of 1954), when it was understood that ministers, since they had no choice but to live very near their churches, should get a benefit.

I decided to see what it would take to become a tax preparer. I asked friends if they or clergy they knew would be interested in these services. (Apparently, this is called market research—who knew?)

I was deeply, deeply skeptical that I could make this work as a business. How much training would I need to do, and how much would that cost? The answer was some training: a sixty-hour course offered by the California Tax Education Council, which also met the requirements to join the Annual Filing Season Program, a voluntary program the IRS runs to encourage better-trained preparers. (Terrifyingly, there are no requirements at all in most states for someone to prepare taxes for others.)

With the fees for the class, a bond, certification with California authorities, and specialized tax software, my overhead was not insignificant, but it was an amount we could manage. Most of the cost went on a credit card with the hope that it would be paid off with money from the upcoming tax season.

Would people really want my services? Yes!

In the first year, I had more than twenty clients; having an already-established network of ministerial colleagues proved to be a great client pool. Still, a reality check—after expenses, I didn't make much money the first year. I did learn a lot. I made some mistakes, corrected them as best I could, and kept on learning.

My small business, Chalice Tax, provides tax consultation and preparation specifically for members of the clergy, who face the aforementioned host of special, unusual tax rules. I'm on the phone with clients often, talking through tax questions, explaining the intricacies of clergy issues, or getting that last piece of information to complete a return.

Clergy face all the challenges every taxpayer does and more. I have clients who come to me unsure how much they owe or don't, clients who haven't filed their returns in years, clients who would rather do almost anything than talk about their taxes, and clients who feel fairly confident but want a tax professional to look it over.

Community ministers face even more challenges than their parish colleagues on the tax front. The community ministers' employers, especially if they're a chaplain or working for a nonprofit, may be both unfamiliar with clergy taxes and unwilling to help the minister access benefits like the housing allowance.

What I didn't expect were the reactions: the crying (either in relief or frustration), the nervous voices, the sighs of relief at having someone they could trust to help deal with this. The best stories are the ones I can't tell; they're confidential and involve personal details about my clients. But I've been stunned at the trust they offer me, giving me a window into deeply personal and private parts of their lives. I hope I have honored that trust, providing them with competent services at a reasonable price. As I sometimes tell my clients, the pastoral care for their tax issues is free.

Last summer, there was a day where I turned in keys at the Napa Valley Unitarian Universalists, where I had just finished doing contract work. I worked there part-time for about twenty months after their previous minister retired suddenly for health reasons, so that they could have time to decide what to do about finding a more permanent minister. It was a successful and rewarding ministry and I was sad to leave it in many ways, though also relieved to be back to working just two jobs, not three.

After turning in my keys, I drove down to the Unitarian Universalist Church of Berkeley to check in with staff and print some important documents. I then went off to the airport to catch a flight to Salt Lake City, where I was to host a two-day retreat for a ministerial search committee that was just beginning its work.

While in the parking lot of the Oakland airport, I had a thirty-minute phone call with one of my tax clients, furiously using the calculator on my phone to try to do some quick tax estimates for him. It was not my preferred working venue, but I made it work—and in bivocational ministry, making it work is often the name of the game.

While that particular summer day may be an extreme example of ministerial multitasking, there are many days that aren't so different. I am often planning worship or meeting with staff and lay leaders at the congregation I serve in the morning, taking a call about someone's taxes in the afternoon (yes, often while providing much pastoral care), and emailing a reply to a search committee somewhere in the western United States in the evening.

My work straddles the worlds of parish ministry, entrepreneur-ial ministry, and community or institutional ministry. My work in the congregation is perhaps the easiest for people to understand—I preach, work with staff and lay leaders, provide pastoral care to peo-ple in crisis, and officiate rites of passage.

My tax business is entrepreneurial: I am solely responsible for my business and for seeking out clients, doing work for them, and getting them to pay me, all of which can be exhausting. Here, too, I am constantly using ministerial skills and trying to help ease the lives of clergy so they can go do their ministries instead of worrying about tax returns.

And the work I do as a regional transitions coach with search committees is entirely different. It is what's known as institutional or organizational ministry; I am an adjunct staff member of the Pacific Western Region of the Unitarian Universalist Association. I mostly work with committees on process: how to navigate the search pro-cess, how to work with candidates, how to involve the congregation as much as possible, and how to pace themselves in what is essentially a part-time volunteer job.

For me, all of this is ministry. Defining ministry isn't easy, espe-cially in today's world, where technology, societal and family norms, and economic realities are changing rapidly. I doubt anyone would argue my parish work isn't ministry. But is my tax work "ministry"? What about my work as a regional transitions coach? You certainly don't need to be ordained to do either, but I do think you need min-istry skills.

For me, ministry is about acknowledging people as fully human, communicating good news to those who are struggling, and holding onto a vision of a world that seeks justice and compassion, not wealth and power. Ministry is more about how we perceive the work we do and how we interact in the world than where our paycheck is coming from or whether others perceive us as ministers. Perhaps that is easy for me to say, as someone who has considerable privilege from both my identity as a cisgender, straight white man, and my professional work as a senior minister of a midsize congregation. But making money is a real concern, and having credentialing bodies and the general public acknowledge your ministry truly matters too.

All of my privilege means I'm rarely questioned about my authority, or at least not questioned *because* of my identities. I have been able to find reasonably good jobs, and as a parish minister, I can go out into the world with the explicit support of my congregation. In contrast, community ministers often find themselves defending the ministry they do and convincing others of its worth. Ministers—both parish and community—who hold marginalized identities face even tougher challenges in receiving and exercising ministerial authority and in getting adequately compensated for doing so.

If I weren't ordained and fellowshipped (that is, credentialed by officials in my tradition), would my tax work be considered a ministry? It's not clear to me that it is considered a ministry, even with my credentials, and that's okay, at least to me. I have my parish work, which has allowed me to be known as a minister and to get through a fairly difficult credentialing process. For ministers doing community and entrepreneurial work without that instant credibility of a parish, things are harder.

And for those of us who aren't independently wealthy, how do you make a living doing ministry now? In a rapidly changing world, bivocationalism is one potential answer. Anyone considering ministry needs to consider what the practical and financial realities of that decision will be, including years of expensive schooling, compensation that can range from extremely meager up to comfortable (though by no means wealthy), the awareness that your time and energy will not always be your own, and the acknowledgment that your vocation and personal life will often be in competition. Being deeply in debt, struggling to make ends meet, and constantly busy does not help create good ministries. Finding ways to balance our work, lives, and health does.

Ministry is a strange calling. I have yet to meet the clergyperson who thinks they have a normal, everyday job. For many of us, the hours are difficult and irregular, though sometimes quite flexible too. In a very real sense, our offices are the entire communities in which we serve.

I have wrestled with what a *sense of call* means. I have colleagues who felt firmly called to ministry, who've had a sense of being pushed or pulled—not always willingly—toward it, or who've had dreams or visions of their future ministry. I've never had those experiences, but I have felt a sense of congruence when it seemed that what I was doing, or thinking about doing, was the right thing for me. If that's a calling, then I certainly felt one about ministry.

On the other hand, I can't say I ever felt a calling to tax preparation. But what I did see was something I was interested in that could not only help people but also help me make a living. There was a market opportunity, as they say in the business world—one that I could fill. Is that a calling? Maybe. I certainly believe people can be called to things other than religious service.

For me, combining tax work, parish ministry, and the occasional other opportunity, like transitions coaching, was a financial necessity as much as it was any calling. A long line of religious professionals have felt similar pressures; many people in general are also feeling those pressures, probably more than in some past times. We hear about teachers working part-time jobs to make ends meet or people stringing together multiple minimum-wage positions and gig-economy jobs just to make enough to cover their bills. Positions that were once seen as middle-class are no longer so in our increasingly stratified, capitalist society, where a few have almost unimaginable amounts of wealth and many have very little.

There is often a stereotypical picture of a clergyperson who spends all week meeting with congregants and preparing for worship: They're full-time, can usually be found in their study at church, and make a comfortable, though not extravagant, living.

The reality is and has always been more complicated. Various religions and denominations have different ideas about what clergy should be and how—or even if—they should be compensated for their work. But even in traditions that have paid clergy, not all communities could support a full-time person. In today's world, bivocational clergy are common. Studies show that somewhere between 10 and 25 percent of US congregations have part-time clergy. Bivocational ministry isn't some strange aberration but rather a fairly common occurrence, and probably more so in smaller congregations and more remote areas. There have always been clergy who were bivocational—that is, priests, ministers, pastors, rabbis, and other religious professionals who do religious work, unpaid or modestly paid, and part- or full-time other work to make a living. The Christian apostle Paul famously made a living by sewing fabric into tents (so much so that the term *tentmaker* has come to refer to all religious professionals who primarily make money outside of religious work), while his religious work was not always paid or only paid meagerly.

There are also people who are bivocational by choice. For me, it was a combination of factors. Being bivocational offers me the chance to have greater flexibility in my schedule to be with my children, to work with my wife in a way that might not be possible otherwise, and to pursue other interests. For others, it's important to have at least part of their working life in the secular world in order to stay grounded and close to their community, or because they love the religious work they do but know that their particular circumstances don't allow it to be full-time.

One of my most important learnings has been that skills from ministry are both useful and desperately needed in so many places. My tax business, other than that it serves clergy, might seem to be fairly disconnected from ministry. On one level, I simply take documents from people, ask them some questions, and fill out their tax return, and in some cases it really is that simple. But often there is so much more!

Clergy taxes are notoriously weird. The rules are simply different from virtually any other type of employment, and consequently, clergy tax returns are often done wrong by well-intentioned but misinformed people. Ministers often don't know the rules, and neither do church treasurers and bookkeepers, though they may be fully qualified in most financial matters. Even payroll companies and tax professionals, if they haven't dealt with clergy before, can be at a loss. This means a lot of potentially costly mistakes are made, and that's often when clients call me.

When I started the tax business, it became clear that this was very much a ministry—and often one of pastoral care. So many people came to me with huge anxiety, about owing money or potentially owing money, about feeling overwhelmed by taxes in general and clergy tax rules in particular, about queasy feelings that they may not have been paying their taxes correctly for years.

I have counseled clients going through divorce, those who owe thousands of dollars in back taxes, clients who get one of those scary letters from the IRS (inside info: the vast majority of IRS audits come in the form of letters, asking for clarification or trying to clear up a discrepancy, and they're generally nothing to be scared of). At least once a month or so, someone comes to me with a question that I have never heard before and that I get to do some research on and try to answer, and those are some of my favorite times. It's similar to the work that goes into preparing a sermon: studying and research, contemplation and integration.

I hope that my clergy role helps clients feel they can trust me, both with their taxes and some of their personal stories. I know that my work in having a non-anxious presence—that is, projecting an unruffled demeanor that can help those feeling anxiety calm down—has helped immensely as I work with tax clients. My previous career, as a reporter and editor for newspapers, also helps. The interviewing skills I learned there often help with tax clients: that almost intuitive knowing what question to ask can be vital. Community ministry is about bringing the gifts we have and the skills we have learned in our lives to the work of healing souls, seeking justice, and transforming the world. We don't leave behind who we are when we enter the ministry. We use who we are to do this work.

My goal is not only to do a professional job of preparing taxes, but also to ease any anxiety or concern my clients have about the process, and even about paying back taxes (more inside info: the IRS offers monthly payment plans with relatively low interest and will work with you to set a payment you can afford).

In both tax work and ministerial work, confidentiality is paramount. I don't talk about what's going on in my congregants' lives, except in very limited instances and with their knowledge and permission. Similarly, I don't talk about my tax clients, not even who they are, much less their situation. A tax client mentioned to my wife the work I had done for them once, and she expressed surprise; the client had assumed I might mention it to my spouse, but I simply don't do that.

The work I learned about in seminary and in parish ministry of having a clear vision and working towards it has also helped in my tax business. My goal with clients is to help them keep perspective: yes, owing money to the IRS is not great, but we can work to see if the amount owed can be reduced or to seek payment plans. No matter what, it's less important than many other things in life, even if it can be overwhelming in the moment.

So many things in our life are like that: our endeavors can lead to failure, but most failure won't destroy you. I'm inspired by community ministers in our faith who are taking big chances, doing new things, failing and trying again, often on a shoestring budget. They make me more brave.

Visioning and goal setting have also helped my tax business: I set goals each year that I hope to achieve. Those goals are usually around increasing my client base and income, but also about how I want to spend my time (tax season can involve some very, very long days) and how this work is contributing to my larger life and that of my family.

The other thing my tax business taught me about ministry was the power of saying yes. I admit I've tended toward caution in my life, avoiding lots of risk and keeping all my options open. But the success, moderate though it is to date, of my tax business has driven me to be more adventurous in the parish. I have pushed for ideas that I might have been more lukewarm on in the past. I have used my authority to speak out more boldly than I might once have done.

The truth is that our congregations are, or should be, much safer places to fail than almost anywhere else. If my tax business fails, I could face significant, though ultimately manageable, consequences: debt, broken relationships with clients, even litigation. I know this is true for other entrepreneurial community ministers in areas like spiritual direction and coaching. In the congregation, I have a community of support to hold me in my failure. And most of the time, failures in congregational life just mean that we put our time and resources towards something that doesn't work out.

The hardest struggle in my work has been finding balance. I love and enjoy doing different things, even all on the same day. It's one of the things that attracted me to parish ministry: just the sheer variety of it all. I get to do different things almost every day, which makes me excited and plays to my skills; I'm good (but not great) at a lot of different things. I know people who are amazing at certain skills and tasks but struggle mightily to balance competing priorities, and what I do wouldn't work for them.

But it's a simple fact that it is more complicated and time-consuming to have two half-time jobs than one full-time job. One-half plus one-half doesn't always equal one, at least in this case. It is simply more work to do two half-time jobs, and sometimes you don't get all the benefits of full-time work either. Vacations are harder to plan, if you can do them at all. In my tax business, I'm my own boss, but I also don't have anyone to help!

I don't want it to sound like I'm constantly busy, because I do take time to recover, and there are certainly busy seasons and more spacious time in all the work I do. I also couldn't do this without the support of my wife, both in our professional life as co-ministers and in our family life.

Technology has made things possible that weren't even a few years ago. My tax business has clients in more than 20 states, and all of my interaction with them is via phone or computer. The business I run wouldn't have existed 20 years ago in anything like the form it does. Tax businesses used to be almost all storefronts, but now many of them are entirely virtual, like mine, or use temporary office space solutions and home offices together.

In my particular situation, I get to experience the best and worst of radically different job situations. The parish work has great rewards: a community of wonderful people I get to see every week; a steady paycheck and benefits; a team of co-workers. It also has challenges: it can feel like everyone wants something different from you (and they want it now!); parish positions are tied to a particular place and situation, and ministerial tenures average only a few years.

My tax business, similarly, has its own rewards: a lot of flexibility; the ability to decide how, when, where and for whom I will work; and a busy season balanced with a lot of relative down time. And it has challenges: I don't have any co-workers to lean on for support; I don't get employer-paid benefits; and it's entirely on me to seek new clients and retain the ones I have.

It's not easy. I think most people who had easier options would probably take them. I'm not at all certain that I will continue doing this bivocational thing forever. But it's possible, it can work, and if it makes sense for you, it can be powerful and sustaining, either for a time or for a lifetime.

"The future of ministry is bivocational." As a seminarian, I heard this from a parish minister at a panel designed to give those of us in ministerial formation wisdom from already credentialed and serving ministers. I noted that he was not bivocational and seemed to have no interest in being so. It was clear that he intended this as a warning to us, but it can also be an opportunity.

The truth is that the future of ministry is already here, and its most notable feature is its diversity. Community ministries, our catchall term for any ministries that don't take place primarily in a congregation, are as diverse as they come, and take place just about anywhere you find people. In the UUA, more than half of all new ministers each year are planning to go into some form of community ministry.

It's not totally clear that ministry is becoming more bivocational, since it always has been that way for some. Perhaps more clergy will be bivocational in the future, but the world is changing so much that any good predictions are hard to make.

Nevertheless, here's my prediction: all of us will need more of the skills required in different forms of ministry. Parish ministers will need more entrepreneurial skills, ever trying out new ways to do things, finding new streams of revenue, and seeking new relationships. Community ministers, even in more specialized roles like chaplaincy, will need to learn the work of leading a community, delegating work, and casting a vision. Institutional ministers will be providing more pastoral care and engaging technology even more.

I remain amazed each time I think about my own path, which has taken twists and turns I never could have planned some twelve years ago when the idea of being a minister first entered my mind, heart, and soul. I am also sure that I can't confidently say where the next twelve years will take me.

For many of us, the future will be bivocational, and that doesn't have to be a scary thing. It can mean working in diverse communities and being a part of knitting them closer together. It can mean finding creative ways to live your passion and have a living wage. It can mean doing what you feel called to do in a way that you never imagined. It can mean serving people who have been ignored by more conventional ministries.

Our ministries are desperately needed in this hurting world. We need people who are willing to challenge established norms of what ministry is and what it can and should be. My advice is to be more brave, more confident in yourself, more creative in seeking out opportunities, and more willing to fail.

Whatever weird idea you're thinking of? Go find out if it's possible. The world needs your ministry, however unconventional it may be.

Q&A with Rev. Amy Beltaine

Would you tell us about the facets of your work and ministry?

I am a spiritual companion doing spiritual direction work. Many people still use the term spiritual director, which is an older Catholic term. My work is primarily over Zoom, so I meet with seekers all over the world. I completed my two-year training with Namaste and received that certificate in 2011. My classmates and colleagues are spiritual companions. That is my identity.

My work is to create a sacred space where people seek and find their spiritual direction. I support and witness people as they develop their relationship with what they hold holy. Sessions often include discernment, the work of deciding what is right for you.

Spiritual companioning is different from counseling, from pastoral care, and from coaching. A therapist or counselor works—though not exclusively—from a healing-brokenness perspective. A spiritual companion knows you are whole, holy, and good. I get in there with seekers as they make meaning of a spiritual experience, or grapple with the loss of spiritual community, or travel through a dark night (or even year!) of the soul.

Rev. Amy Beltaine (she/her) provides spiritual mentoring ministry through individual and group appointments, Sunday services, rites, and rituals. A graduate of Meadville Lombard School for the Ministry, Amy is on the coordinating committee of the UU Spiritual Direction Network and is chair of the spiritual direction program at Cherry Hill Seminary.

Spiritual direction often spans years versus short-term pastoral care. Unlike a coach, a spiritual companion reflects and names truths but doesn't give assignments or advice.

Each spiritual companion, and really, each community minister, has a particular focus or context in which they work. I seek to serve those who crave a world of love and justice—whose wells of nourishment run dry, who wish to break open instead of break down. Together, we seek that which gives life.

Spiritual companioning is well known in Catholicism, but exists in Buddhist, Sufi, Jewish and other traditions. It affirms my panentheistic path because we celebrate each person as they find their own path in partnership with their understanding of the divine. Companions need to be grounded in our own path, and there is no proselytizing, no assumptions, no judgment.

In addition to one-to-one appointments, I offer group workshops and group spiritual direction. I also offer supervision for spiritual directors, which is incredibly important. Every spiritual companion should see a supervisor regularly. I am the lead for a spiritual direction training program affiliated with Cherry Hill Seminary. It is delightful to nurture budding spiritual companions who represent many varieties of earth-relating and deities-honoring perspectives. In February 2022, I received the Wendy Griffin Professor of the Year Award.

What was the process of establishing your ministry like for you?

Apparently Alicia Ford, the MFC coordinator at the time, understood that I was the first spiritual companion to go through the Ministerial Fellowship Committee process, though I don't know if that's true.

My process was smooth. I had Rev. Dr. Hope Johnson in my ear, saying, "You are you. What you are doing is your calling, and they need to deal with it." Hope was my internship supervisor at Unitarian Universalist Congregation of Central Nassau (UUCCN).

When you are a trailblazer, having a mentor with gravitas in your corner is critical to counter what is considered *real* ministry.

I could not have done it without her. That's the bottom line. Since I went through fellowship, the MFC has started asking for business plans and budgets. I have issues with that. I don't think the money you earn is a valid measure of the value of anyone's ministry. Maybe they want to be sure you can eat, but it needs to be clear that they're not measuring the value of a ministry in dollars.

In a parish, the board is the minister's supervisor. I had to ask myself, "Who is my supervisor if I'm not in a parish? Who belongs on the Committee on Ministry if I'm not in a parish?" Find people who are actually in your line of work or who you will be serving. They will absolutely help you in your work.

Your ministry is *your* ministry. Having the courage to claim it is powerful and necessary.

In your view, what is the role of community ministry in the world now?

The institutions we thought were going to last forever are not. We're looking at climate chaos and the economic effects of this. Neighborhood relationships and small congregations are going to be "the thing"—bar church, cabaret church, and being in a community organization where spiritual work gets done.

There are non-profits and businesses where someone is tasked to care for the spiritual well-being of the employees.

Community ministers created entrepreneurial ministry, though I don't know that I love the word because it's embedded in capitalism. We need to create new ways instead of relying on capitalism.

Community ministers are the trailblazers and exemplars of that creativity and are giving us all more options.

What encouragement, advice, or warnings would you give to those considering a call outside the parish?

In this unfolding world, the idea of being able to affiliate with an institution that will take care of you is disappearing. It's a throwback.

As you think about ministry, you need to be thinking about how you are going to keep body and soul together, and that means paying attention and learning how to manage your budget and market—this goes for any ministry, including congregational. We need to reframe how we take financial care of ourselves, from the capitalist economic system to a heart-centered economy, which is part of our mission as ministers and especially part of our work as ministers outside of traditional work. Go learn heart-centered business. That may mean going to traditional business classes or mentors and then translating a heart-centered way for yourself.

There is a myth that if you're doing spiritual work, you shouldn't care about money. I wish I had learned before I started that you need to have a part-time job while you start your practice. You need to be able to talk about money with your clients and not be embarrassed. I wish I had learned about taxes and how to care for my needs.

Anything else you want people to know about this work?

In this time of global climate chaos and disintegration of social structures, we need people who will journey with us more than ever.

I don't think it's a surprise that spiritual companioning has broken out of the Catholic walls. There are Pagan, atheist, and other people offering spiritual direction. We all need that kind of support.

The Artistry of Endings

Rev. Erik W. Martínez Resly

A sanctuary is what I long for. What I am.
—Mazaré Rogers, leader at The Sanctuaries

The Sanctuaries has always been about the people. On a special night in Washington, DC, in December 2019, our people gathered to celebrate and say goodbye.

"We've got those mashed potatoes!" Ahmane' Glover hollered, bouncing with the beat behind her. The two cajón drums struck an intricate yet full-bodied rhythm, accentuated by the occasional tap of the Persian daf, a frame drum delicately balanced in Thalib Razi's left palm. "Strawberry cake," Ahmane' shouted, her face glowing with the joy of improvisation. In between spoken-word exclamations, Anju Madhok softly echoed back the phrases in song, elongating the *aw* in *strawberry*, pulling the tune into a major key that was as sweet as the cake itself. The tambourine shook furiously with anticipation. "Get in line," Ahmane' continued, gesturing to the gawking,

Rev. Erik W. Martínez Resly (he/him) is the founder and former codirector of The Sanctuaries, a multifaith community in Washington, DC, that equipped artists to advance social change. He continues to work on advocacy communications at the American Civil Liberties Union of Texas.

swaying, clapping crowd to follow her directions and not just dance to them—to no avail. Hasan Bhatti pulled a series of chords on their guitar that reverberated throughout the large hall as Arvind Venugopal pounded the keys in a spontaneously choreographed display of mutual appreciation. "Get in line, get in line, get in line—it's feasting time!"

Across the room, Ahmad Abumraighi shuffled through stacks of small prints, each emblazoned with Arabic letters laced together in a delicate, tangled intimacy. On the white T-shirt that slouched off the corner of his table, the words of Palestinian-Egyptian poet Tamim Al-Barghouti took flight, forming the shape of a bird:

In Jerusalem, despite successive calamities / a breeze of innocence and childhood fills the air / And you can see doves fly high / announcing, between two shots, the birth of an independent state.

Two tables down and worlds away, Penny Gamble-Williams gave voice to her own native lands. The tall wooden easel behind her displayed a looming canvas tattooed with dramatic patterns and dynamic colors drawn from her Chappaquiddick Wampanoag heritage, each whispering in their own way of the Great Spirit that inspired them. The stark black-and-white illustrations on the table in front of her hid ancestral memories in the twists and turns of her pen. Some concealed feathers and flowers in the lush sprawl of abstract shapes, while others partially revealed faces, eyes strong and dignified, peering through inky puddles to another world that might still be possible.

Amidst the revelry of sights and sounds, I almost forgot that we had gathered to mark the ending of The Sanctuaries in this form.

On Beginnings

The Sanctuaries is a real-life manifestation
of what I've spent years, silently and
generally on my own, wishing existed.
—Priya Parrotta Natarajan, founding leader of The Sanctuaries

We had a lot to celebrate. In the seven trying yet transformative years since we first started what would become The Sanctuaries, our community had grown from a handful of neighbors gathering in someone's living room to create poems out of newspaper clippings into a nationally renowned training community that has equipped hundreds of multifaith artists with the knowledge, tools, and support to work on the front lines of social change.

The Sanctuaries was born in Washington, DC, which, like so many other cities across the country, is a place of layered contradiction, at once demographically diverse yet socially segregated. While it remains a historically and majority Black city, the ravaging forces of cultural gentrification and socioeconomic displacement are quickly turning "Chocolate City" into more of a white mocha. Consequently, neighborhoods are becoming more transient, their histories disappeared by new narratives of *revitalization*, which further heightens racial mistrust and strains class disparities. One of the lasting byproducts of this storm is a deep sense of isolation. In 2012, before our community began to officially gather, I met in coffee shops and bars with young people from across the region. Some were recent transplants, others multigenerational Washingtonians. I was surprised by how often I would hear people speak of disconnection—they either longed for belonging in a new city or lamented the loss of it.

To my disappointment, as a recently minted minister, the young people I met weren't looking for a rigorously researched and carefully crafted sermon. "I'm good, I listen to podcasts," one of my inter-locutors memorably quipped. As our conversation unfolded, how-ever, that same young person went on to confess that she didn't have any friends with whom she could discuss the podcasts she listened to, or, more generally, any of the deeper questions weighing on her soul. Alongside twenty or so other founders, she worked with me to organize sacred spaces, or "sanctuaries," in pole-dancing studios and barbershops and living rooms, where people of different backgrounds could gather before or after work to share stories and build trust.

Within three years, our community had significantly changed. The leaders of our community had come to realize that our most engaged participants shared a passion for creative expression, so we shifted the focus of our programming to center the arts as spiritual practice. This, in turn, spawned groups of artists who would frequent local open mics, sell handmade jewelry at pop-up markets, even record original songs that racked up tens of thousands of listens. As more and more people learned about our unique fusion of art and soul, we started to attract a much wider demographic, from devout Muslims and evangelical Christians to queer anarchists and New Age Burners. We were also approached by dozens of community activists and national institutions eager to collaborate with our visual, performing, and literary artists on projects to bridge social divides and promote social change.

In one project, for example, six of our artists collaborated with vendors at *Street Sense* who were living on the streets. Over many months, they conceived, designed, and launched a mobile bus exhibit entitled "Street Soul: The Human Side of Homelessness." The inter-active installation wove stories of homelessness into a multisensory and multimedia experience of chaos, anxiety, fear, loss, and ever-present threads of hope. Viewers crouched beneath shards of fore-closed homes bound in bright yellow tape, grasped for dangling strings of keys just beyond reach, and peered through dream catchers to future aspirations of stability. Before exiting, participants were invited to take a zine with action steps for addressing systemic poverty. The educational exhibit traveled across the city on a refurbished school bus, reminiscent of the migratory nature of being unhoused.

In another project, almost a dozen of our artists worked with multiple partners, including leaders at grassroots-organizing powerhouse Empower DC. The creative place-keeping initiative was focused on Ivy City, a rapidly gentrifying neighborhood in northeast Washington, DC. As developers sought to rebrand the area to invisibilize Black life and attract new residents, most poignantly captured by a story in the *Washington Post* that dubbed Ivy City "the next cool DC neighborhood you have never heard of," we endeavored to resist this colonizing narrative by equipping the neighborhood to speak for itself. We initially taught local youth how to screen print yard signs, then canvassed the streets and distributed the signs, photographing long-time residents of all ages as they personalized their signs with words describing their relationship to and aspirations for Ivy City. Combining these photos with archival footage of the neighborhood, we worked with the youth and other community members to fabricate a three-dimensional, five-foot-by-twenty-foot screen-printed, plywood installation, which spelled out IVY CITY. Prior to the official launch, we placed each of the freestanding letters in different locations around the neighborhood, including in the lobby of a luxury apartment building that catered to affluent transplants. At our public unveiling event, over two hundred residents and community stakeholders celebrated the shared heritage of and vision for Ivy City through on-site screen printing, free T-shirts, food, and performances by local artists. In the words of one local resident, the campaign "stirred the soul of Ivy City."

In the process of these and other projects, I witnessed how the communities most impacted by social injustices were speaking out, but their solutions were not being heard. Our work up until that point had primarily focused on documenting their fights; we had been less successful at preventing their further displacement. We needed to develop more impactful strategies—not to give people a voice, but to amplify the voices they already had.

So, in 2017, the members of The Sanctuaries chose to incorporate as a 501(c)(3) nonprofit to secure funding and organizational partnerships that would enable us to train spiritually grounded artists as socially engaged leaders. Unless artists could work alongside other community stakeholders to define the problems facing their community as well as develop strategies to remedy them, they'd have limited influence on the implementation of those strategies after the fact.

The intensive program we designed answered both a need and a hunger. We recruited emerging local artists of different backgrounds, art forms, and justice issues in each cohort, often receiving so many applications that we could only accept 10 percent of applicants through a multistep assessment process that engaged more established artists, organizers, and elders. Once accepted, artists in each cohort embarked on a unique four- to eight-month journey, using personal practice, group reflection, and daylong workshops to develop their critical consciousness, spiritual grounding, artistic versatility, and strategic analysis of how to use arts and culture to affect social change. Throughout the program, artists worked together to apply their learning to an actual grassroots campaign through a praxis model of action-reflection.

As the program grew, so did our resources, and we were finally in a position to hire additional paid staff. Rather than build out our support staff, we made the decision to move towards a co-directorship model of senior leadership, which felt particularly important as a multicultural, multifaith, and multiartistic community. We championed collaboration between our artists as a way to mitigate individual limitations and amplify personal strengths. Now, we could institutionalize that commitment throughout the entire organization.

Ahmane' Glover breathed new life into The Sanctuaries. Her extensive organizing experience and fierce poetic artistry allowed me to deepen my focus on pastoral companionship, fundraising, and campaign strategy, among many other responsibilities. Decisions took longer than before, but the outcomes were always better as a result of our collective discernment. We disagreed regularly and cherished that as proof that we still needed each other. Most importantly, we grounded our co-directorship in spiritual practice and care for one another. That made all the difference.

Over the following two years, we trained and deployed multifaith artists on the front lines of grassroots organizing, civic engagement, and public advocacy campaigns. Our artists designed a series of bilingual visual tool kits to educate low-income families on how to advocate for their rights and well-being through the Healthy Housing Collaborative; coached a spoken-word poet and domestic violence survivor through the process of recording a television PSA with the DC Coalition Against Domestic Violence; used screen printing to secure legal representation for refugees through the Dulles Justice Coalition; championed the dignity of American Muslims in the face of anti-Muslim hate on national platforms at the Smithsonian Institution; produced a new visual narrative for the Women's March that centered queer people of color; supported the first youth-led Climate March and worked with Greta Thunberg and Amnesty International to advance the global Fridays for Future movement; in addition to many other campaigns that impacted over one hundred thousand people in Washington, DC, and beyond.

In the words of Naomi Chandel Kumar, a graduate of our Art for Social Impact training program, "The Sanctuaries is the safest space I've ever been a part of: strangers coming together because we believe in art as a revolutionary tool to better the world."

On Endings

Ninety percent of the things that I experienced
were not what I had originally intended.

—Osa Obaseki, co-chair of The Sanctuaries Board of Directors

Amidst so much life, there was also so much death—on our social media feeds, in the communities we worked in, and in the personal lives of our artists. As liberatory feminist scholar bell hooks reminds us, "All the worship of death we see on our television screens, all the death we witness daily, does not prepare us in any way to face dying with awareness, clarity, or peace of mind."

Dr. Ira Byock, a palliative care physician who works with patients at the end of their lives to die well, attributes this unpreparedness to a misguided understanding of death itself. Throughout his childhood and even into medical school, "Death was always treated as a problem," reduced to a collection of diagnoses to be vanquished, and anything but complete victory spelled personal failure.

I suspect this is as common for religious communities as it is for many of the people who comprise them. During the summer after my graduation from divinity school, in a dark room nestled in the basement of Dallas Theological Seminary, I charted the victorious trajectory of my hypothetical church using Post-it Notes and an oversized roll of newsprint. I drafted each stage of formation along the discipleship process and identified its corresponding organizational benchmarks. This weeklong boot camp had church planting down to a science. Before I even stepped into the field, I was supposed to have a plan for when we would gather, what I would teach, and how far we had progressed according to the biblical timeline for church growth.

"Once you have eighty regular attendees, you're ready to officially launch," our teacher insisted.

I never learned about what happens afterward—after our congregation of eighty grows to eight hundred and we launch satellite campuses across the city, begin livestreaming our services around the world, publish best-selling books, and headline stadium-sized conferences. Catalytic growth was the only option. Onward and upward forever!

A business leader in the booming tech sector recently told me that this orientation is hardly unique to a particular strand of evangelical Christianity. Many corporations are highly skilled in the acquisition of other companies, he explained, but few have as much experience, let alone standard methodologies, for knowing how and when to sell off these businesses when they're underperforming or are no longer the right fit. The financial repercussions of waiting too long to sell are extremely high, he confessed—sometimes millions of dollars.

It's hard to build competency in the art of letting go when we're only taught to start things. The popular Acumen introductory course on social entrepreneurship helps participants "discover their passion and path to change the world." The six-week online journey covers a wide range of topics, from developing a framework for measuring impact to determining the most viable revenue engines, and it concludes with a module on bringing your idea to scale.

What it largely overlooks, unfortunately, is life itself. What happens when you get sick while raising venture capital and have to put your idea on hold? What happens when you and your board of directors can't agree on whether to invest locally or expand to other markets? What happens when your key leaders move, or you lose the space you've been renting at a discounted rate, or you learn that a major foundation just funded a national organization to develop the same program down the street?

Our obsession with beginnings obfuscates the artistry of endings.

"When we live fully in the present," bell hooks advises, "when we acknowledge that death is always with us and not just there at the moment when we breathe our last breath, we are not devastated by events over which we have no control." In fact, we might come to realize, much as Dr. Ira Byock did, that "dying [is] as precious as it was painful."

Big Questions

You reassure me that we are all in process—and
that process is just as important as product.
—Kristen Jackson, Woolly Mammoth Theatre Company,
organizational partner

On the heels of the first Hijrah in 615 CE, as the companions narrowly escaped persecution by the Quraysh in Mecca by fleeing to Medina, Prophet Muhammad ﷺ counseled Abu Dharr to "speak the truth, even when it is bitter" (Shu'ab al-Imān 4582). The closer we are to death, it seems, the more honest our truth-telling—to ourselves in particular.

For years, I had been heralded by friends and colleagues for my stewardship of The Sanctuaries. It filled my days, paid my bills, defined my identity. People would approach me at events and enthusiastically inquire, "Hey, aren't you Sanctuaries?" No matter how hard I lobbied against this conflation, no matter how much I promoted shared leadership and resisted a cult of personality, I finally came to accept that our lives were intricately linked. The Sanctuaries was not only my ministry, it was my mood, a model of the world I so desperately wanted to live in.

So it took me a long time to accept that it was time for us to close.

I initially refused to believe that ending was even an option. I worked tirelessly with other leaders to devise strategies to overcome the latest onslaught of challenges: fundraising was demanding more and more time we didn't have, many of our artists had moved away or were showing up less often, campaigns approached us with larger and larger projects that required greater time and talent. With every stage of organizational growth, we confronted different, often unexpected challenges. This was nothing new. But the longer I sat with our current reality, the more present I grew to what *was* and not just what could or should be, the clearer things became. I didn't yet have answers, but I had good questions.

Sustainability

What makes a community sustainable? On retreat in the backwoods of New Hampshire, a mentor of mine had once insisted that amidst our many differences, our community was not socioeconomically diverse because we didn't have any wealthy artists. *What an oxymoron*, I thought. But he was right. I just didn't know where to find them.

Over time, in large part through rather painful networking attempts at elite galleries and expensive philanthropic functions, we did attract members and supporters with access to greater resources. Unfortunately, with few exceptions, their participation tended to be short-lived once they realized that the thrust of our arts-based organizing work threatened the very systems and structures that protected their privilege.

How do disinvested communities fund their own liberation? How do they afford growing staffs to meet the elaborate demands of the nonprofit industrial complex? Or, if they adopt a different model, how do they compete with the breadth and convenience of services that large institutions dangle in front of their constituents, even when these interventions only address symptoms instead of root causes? In a world where money begets money, how do organizations created by and not just for low-income people survive?

One of our last campaigns used street art to prevent opioid overdoses (see the illustration on page 97). I learned of the city's request for proposals through a local clergy listserv, of which the grant administrator was a member. The funding opportunity had just been announced, and the deadline for completed applications was two weeks away. I immediately set up calls with a couple of our closest partners to explore the possibility of submitting a joint proposal, given the massive scope of the project. Simultaneously, I reached out to our artists to gauge interest and availability. A week later, I had secured a committed organizational partner and a team of eager artists. As the grant deadline rapidly approached, in between existing responsibilities that filled my schedule, I scrambled to jointly draft the guiding theory of change, programmatic benchmarks, assessment metrics, budgetary rationale, and reporting timeline that comprised the first section of the application.

That was the easy part. The second section of the application required extensive documentation of the partner organization's legal structure, financial history, and licensing going back generations. We were able to excavate most of the materials in online folders and old filing cabinets, but we realized that one of the documents confirming eligibility for city-funded projects expired every twelve months and needed to be renewed. Just hours before the deadline, I rushed across the city and waited in line to get a copy of this certificate, then jetted off to FedEx to print six hard copies of the eighty-page application before hand-delivering these materials to the receptionist on the second floor of an unmarked government building.

We learned that our proposal had been selected after receiving an email instructing us to show up for a three-hour orientation two days later, in the early afternoon. I rearranged my schedule to accommodate this last-minute mandatory meeting. The session focused on how to educate residents about opioid prevention and treatment using a series of informational materials that were still being final-ized. We were assured that they would be sent to us within a couple days of the start of the grant period. I received the PowerPoint two weeks before the grant period closed.

I share this saga not to disparage city officials but to illustrate the context in which we had to negotiate organizational sustainability. These were the conditions, constraints, and compromises that made this work possible in the first place. I wouldn't have heard about the grant if I hadn't been a member of the clergy. I wouldn't have met the deadline if I didn't have a car to chase after certificates or the hundreds of dollars in our bank account to pay for the printing. I wouldn't have completed the project in the designated time frame if I hadn't been working with people who were willing and able to finalize designs and wheat paste posters and facilitate trainings with less than a week's notice.

We lost far more grants than we won. Most funders opted for breadth over depth. They were intrigued by our vision of equipping artists to navigate the aforementioned process on their own so that we could have more leaders working on more projects to advance social change—but they wanted us to train hundreds of artists in dozens of cities at a time, preferably in a weekend or two. This was the code we couldn't crack: We needed to do the work in order to fund the training of others to do the work, without the time or resources to do both. There came a point when sustainability no longer meant finding a way to endure this endless loop but rather finding a way to move beyond it.

Accountability

To whom is a community accountable? In the wake of Freddie Gray's horrifying death at the hands of the Baltimore police just an hour up the road from us, organizers of the local Black Lives Matter chapter invited our community to co-organize an event. I knew a couple of the leaders personally, as did a number of our artists, so we desperately wanted to show up in support and solidarity.

As the leaders of our community learned more about the details of the event, we faced important questions as an organization. The event was a BIPOC-only space, and we were a multiracial community. We wholeheartedly supported race-based caucusing, affinity groups, and other spaces of this nature, often organizing them within our own community. At the same time, we were cognizant of the fact that we would be co-organizing an event that a subset of our artists couldn't attend. To whom were we accountable, and what did that really mean?

Courtesy of Vy Vu

It might seem straightforward to suggest that a community is accountable to the people who belong to it. But is accountability that simple? What if the community only comprises one racial or generational or class demographic? When does accountability extend beyond those currently gathered? In the aftermath of sweeping gentrification that has pushed entire city blocks into distant suburbs, many neighborhood churches in Washington, DC, that were once overflowing with Black members must now decide whether or not to cater to their new, overwhelmingly white neighbors. What if the needs of the community at hand—or the needs of the community you seek to nurture—do not align with what you can or want to provide?

For months, attendance at The Sanctuaries community gatherings was down, and I couldn't figure out why. Many of our founders had since moved out of the city and others had moved on to pursue other passions, but the majority of our members continued to enthusiastically champion and financially support the organization. We surveyed people about the type of programming they wanted, adjusted schedules, and shifted locations to make gatherings more accessible—we even provided better food. But little changed. Meanwhile, some of the members who did regularly attend our programs were becoming so frustrated by this trend that they stopped showing up as well.

One day, I received a text from Raven Best, a longtime leader in our community who had since gone on to pursue advanced education in graphic design to follow her dreams of becoming a full-time artist. We met for breakfast to catch up. I explained the dip in attendance and invited her insight on how to remedy the situation. She paused, summoned her words carefully, and then said it to me straight: "They no longer need you, Rev."

That was the first time I had considered the possibility that The Sanctuaries had been successful—not in terms of what our artists had accomplished but in terms of who our artists had become. What does accountability mean when a community fulfills its commitment to its people?

As soon as I shifted my focus from what members weren't doing to what they were, the stories began pouring in. One artist was helping to combat ICE's deportations of refugees by filming interviews with organizers, at-risk community members, and their families. One artist was organizing nationwide rallies to protest the unjust military occupation in Kashmir. One artist was using photography to call out corruption through actions with Shut-DownDC. One artist was exploring the ways that fiber arts can be used for creative expression and cultural resistance through public library programming with young people. One artist was developing resources, workshops, and programs that highlight the importance of health, wellness, and healing. Some artists were collaborating on mixtapes or working together on films or just meeting up for brunch. Each effort required time. They chose to attend fewer programs at The Sanctuaries to grow the mission of The Sanctuaries in their lives.

Shortly before the artists' public graduation from our Art for Social Impact training program, Ahmane' organized a community round table where participants in the last cohort of our program could hear directly from members of the community in which they had been learning and working. It was an important form of accountability. We sat in a circle lining the chapel of the Festival Center in Columbia Heights, a venue where we had held so many of our programs over the years. The midafternoon sunlight set the large stained-glass windows ablaze and bathed the entire room in color. One by one, the community members shared what they'd noticed. They appreciated our artists for their talent, commitment, and, above all, their care. Then, one of the community members asked our artists whether they intended to stay engaged in the fight for economic justice.

"Yes!" a graduate snapped.

"I'm here for the long haul," another graduate added.

As we completed the circle, the room filled with pledges of ongoing support, regardless of role or affiliation or compensation. They just wanted to be of support.

In that moment, I felt my role shift. Accountability no longer meant training artists for this sacred work but rather entrusting them with it.

The Sanctuaries had reached a point of commencement. It was time for us to stop training people to do the work so that we could open up new opportunities for people to do the work. Some of us would embed ourselves in other organizations, some of us would deepen our involvement in other campaigns, some of us would continue on the teams we had formed, some of us would integrate everything we had learned into our jobs and relationships and side hustles, and some of us would simply take time to breathe. In the end, we decided that the most sustainable and accountable way to transition into this next phase of our shared ministry was by closing down our institution.

I grieved, I celebrated, I prayed. Birth and death are equally fragile crossings. As Roberto Juarroz writes,

> El fondo de las cosas no es la muerte o la vida.
> El fondo es otra cosa
> que alguna vez sale a la orilla.

> The bottom of things is neither life nor death.
> The bottom is something else
> that sometimes comes out on top.

On Living and Dying

The Sanctuaries saw my flaws and named
them blessings. Saw my tender, vulnerable core
and named it *leadership*. It called me *artist*.
It called me *healer*. It called me *minister*.

—Katie Byron, leader at The Sanctuaries

Nando Álvarez and I had just finished scrubbing sinks, peeling paint, and stacking screens. Most of the screen-printing process is preparation and clean-up; perhaps that's true of life as well. This had become a regular ritual for those of us who called the studio our second home. We loved testing the versatility of the medium. Sometimes, we'd print large-scale, multilayered posters that campaigns could use in public rallies and gift their most ardent supporters. Other times, we'd print black-and-white line drawings on hand-ripped pieces of unbleached muslin that youth could pin on to backpacks and jean jackets as a form of wearable protest. Most of the time, we'd coat the screens, expose the designs, and wash out the emulsion in our studio before packing a car trunk full of supplies so that we could print off-site—meet the people where they are.

As Nando undraped his coat from the folding chair and I switched off the light, an unexpected question bubbled up. "Nando," I asked, "what if The Sanctuaries didn't exist?"

Nando seemed surprised by the question, as was I. It was months before this hypothetical scenario would return as a real possibility. The stillness of the empty studio hid the restlessness of our minds. Glazed by the soft glow of the streetlights outside the window, I could see Nando digging for the words to express his heart. "I—I guess," he stuttered, lifting his eyes from the floor, "I guess I would lose a bit of hope for humanity."

It was a reminder of what's at stake when we do ministry, when we commit our lives to what The Sanctuaries' board member Osa Obaseki calls "that spiritual gangsta shyt."

Midway through our closing celebration at the Festival Center, members of our performance team summoned my co-director and me for a special serenade. As I scanned the large room, Ahmane' wasn't anywhere to be found. I checked the hallway, dashed off to the foyer, even scavenged the closet that housed spare speakers and microphone stands. Nothing. "Check the chapel," someone shouted. I ran across the hall and poked my head into the small circular cove.

There, in the midst of an event that she largely organized, I could see Ahmane' consoling another artist with tears in her eyes.

This was community ministry: the mutual care that we offer one another in and beyond any formal organization.

To close out our celebration later that night, all of us formed a circle around the large room where we had just finished eating dinner. Some artists had flown in from Oakland and driven down from Detroit to be there. It was surreal to be back together. Before I could gesture to Ahmane' to announce our closing ritual, a member stepped into the circle with instructions. "Raise your hand if you're in a different career because of The Sanctuaries." Half of the room raised their hands, then lowered them reverently. "Now, raise your hand if your life has been fundamentally transformed by The Sanctuaries."

Everyone's hand went up. I started to sob.

We always knew that The Sanctuaries was more than a place; it was never confined to a specific building or part of the city. Over time, as artists came and went, we slowly started to accept that it was also more than a specific group of people. But in that moment, for the first time, I finally realized what The Sanctuaries was, at least to me: It was the act of making whole.

Wholeness looks and feels different to everyone. "I found a sanctuary for all the parts of me that needed a home: the artist, the spiritual seeker, the feminist, the leader," Sobia Ahmad, a graduate of our training program, once wrote.

This creating of sanctuary—this inviting all parts to be at home—was always a process rather than a product. It was a verb that each of us would pick up and try on and pass around, for ourselves and for each other.

The closing of The Sanctuaries is not the end of this process but its expansion. It's the quake that shakes hardened parts of ourselves free to be made whole. As I release my role as leader, I'm learning about the artistry of endings and new beginnings, over and over again.

I'm growing a little more into my own wholeness.

Ministry in Liminal Times

Rev. Suzanne Fast

I think of our experiences as raw material from which we make meaning of our lives and our world. Living is an invitation to spiritual transformation and growth. I remember when I was in discernment about leaving my job and community and going to seminary. My minister, Peter Raible, used to say, "Ministry is about growing souls." That spoke to me. Not that a minister can grow souls like a gardener grows cabbages, but that people's souls are transforming. Ministry is about paying attention to that, companioning people as they make meaning of their lives and the world and encouraging them in the work of spiritual growth. We do it when we lift things up in preaching (in person, online, or in print), and we do it when we mark milestones with rites of passage, when we facilitate conversation and exploration, when we sit by a bedside.

My roots are in spiritual direction. Even though I'm doing justice ministry, I come at it with that framework. The thirst for justice is the longing of the soul. It's reflected in the questions I ask: Where is the spirit moving in this work? How is injustice inhibiting the soul?

Rev. Suzanne Fast (she/her) is a Unitarian Universalist community minister focusing on disability justice, advocacy, education, and pastoral ministry. She is particularly interested in the spiritual journeying of adults and children and the connections we make between our inward journeys, our daily lives, and our shared work for a just society.

What do our choices say about our true values? What calls us to be in this struggle?

Author and spiritual director Susan Beaumont says we are in a liminal era. Leadership consultant Sharon Daloz Parks says we are living at the crossroads of wonder and suffering. These are uncomfortable, anxious times of structural change, in and beyond the church. These are also times for experiment, curiosity, creativity—generative times. We will thrive if we embrace the both/and that these times invite. Beaumont suggests it's a time for a ministry of presence. In unclear times, the challenge is to embrace the liminal. Community ministry calls us, as individual ministers and as a faith tradition, to seek where the spirit is moving in the world, build bridges, go beyond our refuges. In encountering the new, we may discern ourselves afresh.

I felt a call to professional ministry for a long time before I followed it. Like so many things of the spirit, it's hard to capture in words what I mean by *call*. Not a literal voice, though the biblical phrasing "still, small voice" resonates with my experience. But something visceral. A metaphorical pull to a particular kind of service in the world: ministry.

We talk a lot about calling in ministry, especially during formation, the time when a minister is going through seminary, internship, and ongoing professional development and discernment. But that's only the half of it. It takes call and response to make a ministry. And responding to my call was not simple.

I became disabled while I was in seminary. The timing was awful. After deciding not to enroll twice before, I had finally committed to following that call, getting a master's of divinity, and pursuing ordination. Instead, I got sicker and sicker and sicker and eventually had to take an indefinite leave from graduate school.

My illness causes chronic pain, which is in itself exhausting. Navigating the medical bureaucracy was bewildering, and I was fortunate to have already done a year of clinical pastoral education—on-the-job chaplaincy training—in a hospital, so I had some familiarity with parts of the system. My husband and I moved from Chicago to Florida, where the climate and physical accessibility was much better for someone with modest means. All the changes consumed every scrap of energy I could muster.

I was fortunate to have a strong personal faith that life is worth living, that it is all grist for the mill. I also had the support of family and friends, and I didn't give much thought to ministry for quite a while. When I did, I thought my capacities were too small to do ministry. I had yet to realize that it was my concept of ministry that was too small. I kept waiting for that sense of call to get with the program and leave me alone.

Meanwhile, I was learning what it meant to be disabled. There are the big things about being invisible and erased by society: It was 1998, I was recently disabled, and, as a longtime TV baseball watcher, I suddenly noticed that the crowd shots always skipped the wheelchair sections of the stadiums, erasing people as efficiently as the so-called ugly laws had done until the mid-1970s. (For two centuries, these laws made it a crime to be disabled or otherwise "unsightly" in public view.) I noticed the 2020 primary season was the first time that most presidential candidates had detailed platforms about disability issues, developed with disability activists. Speaking out against erasure was my introduction to disability activism.

And there are the practical things about accessibility and accommodations. The struggle to vote in Chicago, waiting at the bottom of a ramp for someone to come and unlock the accessible entrance to the church that was my polling place, helped convince me to move where most things were built after the Americans with Disabilities Act. The sad reality is that in 2020, houses of worship remain some of the least accessible places in America.

And there are the spiritual things about accepting who I am and not pining to be someone else. I am deeply rooted in the belief that our inherent worth is not based on productivity. So I was only a little rattled when I heard established colleagues say of my illness, "What a waste," though it always stings. But indeed, I had internalized much of society's fetishization of independence. Learning a much more direct appreciation for the notion of interdependence strengthened my faith and helped better equip me for the struggle for mutual liberation.

In the process of learning to claim disability as essential to my lived experience and my identity, I learned that I could still companion people on their spiritual journey, that I still had a prophetic voice, and that I could still lead. But these things were not what I had thought they were. And I was fortunate that there were people who continued to see the minister in me and who sustained me in the process: colleagues and mentors, laypeople and staff at the Unitarian Universalist Association, Unitarian Universalists and people from other traditions, family and friends and physicians.

With the encouragement of my then-minister, Rev. Kenn Hurto, and fellow ministerial student (now colleague), Rev. Margaret Beard, I enrolled in a three-year, part-time local training program in spiritual direction. That program and its leaders, Kathleen Kelly and Sr. Sallie Latkovich, as well as the Catholic laywomen in my cohort, were all instrumental in my own discernment. I developed an appreciation of my call as dynamic and evolving. Saying yes to the call seemed possible again.

With the support of Rev. Devorah Greenstein and the short-lived UUA Office of Accessibility Concerns, I began to reengage the process of UU ministerial formation. It took many years to complete, but I did. The formation process had to undergo its own changes to embrace a wider concept of what a minister is.

There's nothing new about community ministry. The UU Urban Ministry, which runs programs for children and youth, an emergency shelter for individuals and families fleeing from domestic violence, and job- and education-readiness training for survivors of domestic violence, has been in Boston for almost two hundred years. And yet conventional parish ministry has dominated our concept of what ministry is. Even well-established paths of community ministry—serving as a hospital chaplain, on the UUA staff, or on a seminary faculty—were secondary paths and have been recognized and recognizable based on their similarities to and differences from parish ministry.

These days, so many are being called to community ministry. It is one way that ministry is changing to fit these liminal times. People's relationships to religion and institutions are changing, and the forms of religious leadership are changing too. Many people are creating new ministries from scratch without an established path. Entrepreneurial ministries, bivocational ministries . . . all manner of ministries are blooming. My ministry through EqUUal Access is part of that.

Because of the nature of my disabilities, I have a capacity of about ten hours a week, but those hours don't conform to any predictable schedule. I am not "employable," so my ministry is as a volunteer. I had not set out to do an identity-based ministry. Looking back at my original thoughts when I went to seminary, I thought my call was to some form of chaplaincy or spiritual direction. But EqUUal Access and I have been well-suited to each other and to this time of emerging ministries.

According to its 2012 mission statement, EqUUal Access is "a membership organization of Unitarian Universalists living with disabilities, our families, friends, and allies coming together for a common purpose: to enable the full engagement of people with disabilities in Unitarian Universalist communities and the broader society." Founded in 2008 in support of the UUA Office of Accessibility Concerns, EqUUal Access has primarily been an education and advocacy organization focused on transforming attitudes among non-disabled Unitarian Universalists and in UU institutions. I was an initial member, though not among those who created the organization. I became involved in the leadership in 2010, at about the time the elimination of the Office of Accessibility Concerns was announced.

In these early years, much of our capacity has gone to three main efforts: reaching congregational leaders through workshops and booth conversations at General Assembly; encouraging the UUA and UU institutions to incorporate an anti-ableism lens in their work and illuminating times when the reverse is true; and providing resources to congregations through the Accessibility and Inclusion Ministry Program for congregational certification. My ministry has included work in all those areas.

Because General Assembly gathers so many UUs from so many places—people who are curious and invested in some part of congregational life, whether or not they are currently in a formal leadership role—it is an amazing outreach opportunity for a volunteer organization with a small leadership circle, like EqUUal Access, to spread a message, hear stories, and build relationships that reach across the country and beyond. And it's a great opportunity to partner with other organizations and to build relationships of solidarity. While I initiated most of our General Assembly activities—organizing the booth, developing workshops, networking and advocating in General Session, and addressing ableism as it arises—those activities take new shape as times change and others take primary responsibility.

Much of my time has been spent encouraging people to challenge society's messages that devalue disabled people's lives and to ground that work in UU spiritual values. Society sees disabled people as defective and in need of fixing. This understanding of disability teaches that disabled people are worth less and that the lived experience of disabled people is not important to society. This is the bedrock of ableism that our society indoctrinates in us. But when we take seriously the notion that every person has inherent worth, then disability becomes just another part of the infinite variability of human beings, the foundation for disability rights. When we get comfortable with the notion that we are interdependent—a countercultural value—we give importance to a relational reality that many disabled people are living, and to the principle that everyone's lived experience contributes to the whole. These familiar values call us to a framework which includes access and equity but is justice-centered, liberatory, and intersectional. A framework that is harmonious with the model of disability justice promoted by and centering the voices of disabled LGBTQ+ people and disabled people of color.

As in many ministries, a lot of mine is about meeting people where they are and encouraging them. When most people think about disability, they think about physical accessibility: ramps and elevators, maybe hearing loops. In congregational settings, this gets complicated by shame. I don't give absolution for inaccessible spaces; access *is* important. If disabled people can't participate because of physical barriers, *everyone* loses. But getting in the door is only part of it. Changing attitudes, becoming countercultural to society's notion of disability, is essential work, and for the most part, there is no monetary cost involved, though it does ask us to think and act and speak differently about what it means to be human. In fact, transforming attitudes is often the critical groundwork to making accessibility a priority. Accessibility gets people in the door, but without changing attitudes, we cannot get to justice.

Sometimes my ministry has taken the form of writing articles or creating General Assembly workshops or addressing an issue on the floor of General Session. Sometimes it has meant having conversations intended to make someone with authority uncomfortable and asking for a place at the table for finding a new way. Often, it has been about listening for the movement of the spirit and reflecting it back. Almost always, it has been about cultivating relationships with individuals and organizations so that together we are bringing about a more just Unitarian Universalism and, through that, a more just society. (All of this means I spend a lot of time in meetings and conversations. Since my work is not geographically limited, almost all of these meetings happen through video conferencing, so even before the COVID-19 pandemic put seemingly everyone on Zoom, a good internet connection was essential!)

One of the things I've learned in this ministry is that change at an institutional level usually takes a lot of time. It may seem like it happens in a moment, but that moment is really the tip of an iceberg, and it's easy to miss the years of laying the groundwork that lies beneath the surface. Side with Love was one of those moments.

In 2010, we in EqUUal Access were appalled when the UUA debuted its new coordinated social justice program. It was called "Standing on the Side of Love." It is so common in our society to associate things that are good with nondisabled-body metaphors and things that are bad with disabled-body metaphors that people don't generally even notice. We noticed. We said it was unjust for a justice campaign to reinforce society's biases. But the people making the decisions were enamored with the name, it was associated with an important speech and a beloved song, and a lot of money had been spent on marketing. That was the name, period.

For years, we would go to rallies and cross out the word *standing* on placards and T-shirts, writing in *sitting* or *rolling* or just leaving it as *on the side of love*. We kept saying, again and again in different places and in different ways, that it wasn't alright. That one doesn't need to stand to work for justice—some of the most effective actions for justice were the sit-down strikes of the labor movement, the sit-ins at lunch counters, Rosa Parks refusing to give up her seat on the bus. That, as a faith tradition, we did not have a good record on disability-related social justice, and othering disabled people isn't alright. That if it's "just a metaphor," then find a better one.

Meanwhile, we talked about ableism and inclusion and living our values. We talked about it at General Assembly. We talked about in print, whenever we could get an opportunity. We talked about it one-on-one and in small gatherings. We started a sermon contest, and we started the Accessibility and Inclusion Ministry (AIM) certification program for congregations. We built relationships of solidarity with other folks on the margins.

At the same time, more people were speaking out about ableism in the moment. More people recognized it when it was pointed out. More statements about antioppression remembered to include our community. More disabled folks went to seminary, and more nondisabled folks came out of seminary with an anti-ableist lens.

In 2017, the time was right for change. The campaign itself was ready for a change. Rev. Theresa Ninán Soto shepherded a resolution through the General Assembly, asking to consider a name change.

I remember speaking on the floor of the General Session. I pointed out to the delegates that it was the fortieth anniversary of the Women and Religion Resolution, which had lifted up that imagery that was all-masculine was not, in fact, universal but that it harmfully reinforced negative stereotypes, and called on us to change the language and imagery we used. I asked the delegates to carry on that legacy.

A number of people spoke for the change that day. The delegates voted for the resolution, and the New Year brought in a new name for the campaign: Side with Love, an overnight success that was many years in the making.

As EqUUal Access moves along in its second decade, it is changing. And my ministry is changing too. Some of these changes reflect the modest success we have had challenging societal ideas about disability; some of this reflects the period we are in now in Unitarian Universalism and our changing assumptions about who we are, what lived experiences we bring, and how things work.

It's early to tell, but it seems that one way these changes will show up for EqUUal Access is to broaden our focus. So many of our efforts have been devoted to changing attitudes of nondisabled people. While that work isn't done, it is difficult to sustain outwardly directed work indefinitely without tending to the spirits of disabled people in an intentional way. As other people take up more of the work of accountability and as that work itself changes with changing times and generations, I am excited to turn more of my attention to the work of creating spaces for community worship and reflection and building resilience for the journey.

Because I have to budget my energy so carefully, I am keenly aware of a reality of community ministry off the beaten path: Creating a new ministry and doing that ministry each take time and energy. Doing something where there is no map to follow is taxing. Setting up structures, securing funding, and getting the word out are just a few examples. An initial programmatic approach may need refining and possibly some major overhauls as it takes shape. It is important to pay attention to how much "experi-fail" one can handle. If you are on this path, know your own spiritual, psychological, emotional, and financial bottom lines and revisit them often. Have people with whom you can think things through, people to whom you feel accountable, people who believe in you and your ministry. They don't have to be the same people, though they can be. Prioritize self-care, rest, family (whether biological or chosen), friends, and your own spiritual life. It is much easier to sustain the demands of ministry if you're not drawing from an empty well.

A lot changed from the time I picked up stakes and started seminary in 1993 until I received preliminary fellowship in 2016. *I* changed. Unitarian Universalism and our ministry changed. The world changed. Of course, we are still changing, and meanwhile, I proceed toward full fellowship at my pace.

That I'm allowed and encouraged to proceed at a pace that works with my disabilities is part of a movement of the spirit in our faith: to notice, challenge, and release long-held normative assumptions about who we are as Unitarian Universalists, about our culture, about who can serve in professional ministry and the formation process. If we can stay with this challenge during these liminal times, the formation process will continue to adapt, and our professional ministry will reflect and benefit from the variety of talents and life experiences among us.

Not so long ago, a ministry like mine would not—could not—have been recognized. In part because of my stubbornness and the stubbornness of that call, and in part because of the changing culture of Unitarian Universalism, today I am an ordained and fellowshipped Unitarian Universalist minister. Through the path of community ministry, so many of us are redefining the limits of ministry and claiming our call.

Q&A with
Rev. Chuck Freeman

How did Texas UU Justice Ministry (TXUUJM) get started?

We had an organizational meeting at my previous church, Live Oak UU, in 2012. We organized a steering committee and got eight churches that were our charter members. We ended up getting a quarter-time grant, so I had the reins to be the executive director, and that was heartily accepted. I've been guiding the group since then; 2013 was our first legislative session.

We primarily focus on covenanting with congregations, asking member churches to make a nominal dues contribution to participate. When a congregation covenants with us, they get two people on our advisory council, which is our grassroots connection to our congregations. We have our email list and monthly call with that group to talk about what we're doing collectively and in their congregations. It's a really good time to hear what others are doing, say, "That's a great idea!" and get connected to work together. It's a place for relationships that are grounded in doing justice work in Texas.

Rev. Chuck Freeman is the minister and executive director emeritus of the Texas Unitarian Universalist Justice Ministry, which he co-founded and led for ten years. A UU minister known for his justice activism, he has also served Live Oak UU Church in Cedar Park, Texas, and Free Souls in Round Rock, Texas. This interview was conducted when he was serving as executive director of TXUUJM.

We currently have thirty-six congregations in our coalition. I'd say about twenty-five of those are very active.

What's your workweek like? Is there a typical workweek?

I'm getting paid half-time, and you know the rest of that sentence [laughs]. The Texas legislature meets every other year for 140 days, starting in January, so we have that routine. Our issues are voted on by our congregations. We went through a deliberative ten-week process and ended up focusing on racial justice, environmental justice, health care access, economic justice, and voting rights.

Three of those are very new to us: Racial justice is new as an explicit item for a legislative action. Environmental and voting rights are also new to us as legislative priorities for TXUUJM. We're reaching out to form new allies. Our whole perspective is that it's relational work: You build relationships with allies, legislators, and people in elected positions, even relating to those you don't agree with in a way that's respectful and honors their inherent worth and dignity, even though you may fiercely disagree. We don't demonize or dehumanize them.

Yesterday, I had two or three calls with legislators and their teams, and I have another one this afternoon. I reach out through our board and advisory council, like, *Who do you know? Who are you working with in your community?* But nobody has a good feel for this session because of COVID-19 and very few people being at the Capitol, so it's hard to communicate when people are at home in their districts. It's very disjointed.

I've been a minister in this district since 1996. I go to area minister meetings and retreats. I'm in two congregations every month, speaking, connecting, reaching out, and sending the newsletter. You demonstrate that we're in a partnership by your interests and relationship building.

How does community ministry lead our faith?

To me, that's where our real work gets done. If we're an insular group that just wants a place of sanctuary where we feel safe and everybody believes like we do, we've referred to our congregations like that for years. That's the starting point, but that's not the end point. Too many of our congregations get stuck there, hiding out from all these mean people and becoming a spiritualized social club.

In community ministry, it's important to be partnered with a congregation. You can align with them and help enliven them to their mission and calling. You transform yourself, and that radiates to your families, your congregation, the world, the economic and political structure. As far as I'm concerned, the community ministries are the ones that enliven and really carry out the mission that we're called too.

I always talk about investing. You're investing your time, heart, soul, and finances to express our life-affirming, life-giving values in the world. It's always a partnership. I work pretty hard to not be the focus of attention—more like the point guard, if you want to use a basketball analogy. It's not a top-down operation. We have so many people who are committed to doing the work. There are some things I initiate and direct, but for the most part, it comes from the people and congregations. I join in and add value, using our infrastructure to share how people can get involved and be inspired by the local work and celebrate.

Healing Moments for People with Alzheimer's

Rev. Dr. Jade Angelica

I'm a trauma survivor. Like many other survivors—like many people, actually—I tend to be fearful of the unknown. Because of our fear, we often try to deny unwanted realities or control what happens next in a desperate attempt to know the future. Keith Johnstone, improvisation performer, teacher, and author of *Impro: Improvisation and the Theatre*, calls us "no" sayers. Through our efforts, he says, we experience more safety. Alternatively, "yes" sayers—those who accept what is and are comfortable not knowing what will be—experience more adventure.

In the arena of improvisational theater, Johnstone's assessment may be a primary truth. In the arena of real life, though, another deeper truth about "no" sayers and "yes" sayers emerges: By saying "yes" to what is—by accepting reality and being open to the future rather than fearing it—we can experience more healing. Johnstone proposes that we "no" sayers can learn to say yes, and my own story is a hopeful testament to this possibility.

Rev. Dr. Jade Angelica (she/her) is a UU community minister and spiritual director, offering hope and inspiration for people with Alzheimer's and their loved ones through her writing and workshops. Jade's most rewarding ministry has been caring for her mother, Jeanne, who died from Alzheimer's in 2011.

I discovered improvisation during a truly terrible time in my life. An abusive relationship had ended, and the dividing of our mutually owned property and assets was festering in the courts. My suffering was evident to everyone. Finally, a wise friend suggested that, in addition to my therapy and support group, I might benefit from having some fun. She encouraged me to attend an improvisation class. I'm not sure why or how I actually got myself there, but I went to the class and my life changed forever.

At first, I was terrified. The other students were much younger extroverts with a knack for comedy; many were actors interested in improving their performance skills. I was the only sad, frightened introvert seeking healing. During the first few classes, I cowered in the corner, hoping with all my strength that the teacher wouldn't call on me to participate in an exercise in front of the class. He didn't. After the third class, as I walked alone down the stairs of the studio, I heard a judgmental little voice inside me, proclaiming firmly and sarcastically, *Well, you're certainly getting your money's worth out of this, aren't you?*

That awareness was all I needed to propel me into participating fully in the class—and as my friend predicted, it was such fun!

The camaraderie among classmates, the hilarity, and the cheek-aching laughter facilitated the first level of healing that I experienced. The class raised my energy and resurrected my joy. Soon, however, I began to notice that the principles of improvisation resembled spiritual qualities I had studied in theology classes, practiced through prayer and meditation, and aspired to integrate into my life, qualities such as:

+ Attentive listening
+ Being present in the moment
+ Expanding awareness and observation (mindfulness)

✦ Letting go of the need to control or even know what happens next

✦ Being open to noticing and receiving what the situation is offering (accepting reality)

✦ Responding in a way that is supportive and promotes self-esteem (the first rule of improvisation is to make your scene partner look good)

✦ Acknowledging our interdependence

✦ Opening ourselves up to previously unimagined possibilities

✦ Experiencing, embracing, and expressing joy

During the first series of classes, I discovered through mind-body experiences that embracing these qualities embodied in the practice of improvisation could and did lead me to healing. Much to my surprise, it also led me to the next chapter of my community ministry.

Even attempting to consider that improvisation has healing potential challenges most people, because we think this creative drama craft is about comedy and performance and being outrageously clever or quick-witted—but it's not, or at least it's not only that. At its core, improvisation is about being obvious, saying yes to what is offered, and saying or doing the next logical thing. It's about being authentic and exploring what it means to be human. My first teacher, David LaGraffe in Portland, Maine, shared that he had moved away from improv comedy over the years, focusing on what he called pure improv. He described pure improv as "an unconditional welcoming of the present moment." From this perspective, he said, "Improvisation is not so much inventive as it is revelatory. We learn to trust that everything we need is already here, waiting to be discovered if we are willing to be open to it."

My efforts to heal from my failed relationship led me to the revelations of improvisation and helped me to see my life patterns of resistance and control. Previously, in my "no"-saying life, I used will, skill, and persistence, trying to make situations fit my preferences, especially if I didn't like or want what was happening. But when resistance is implemented in an improvised scene, it's called *blocking the offer*. This is the realm of "no" saying where scared improvisers seek safety or control, and it inevitably leads to a very bad scene.

My resistance became indisputable, even to me, during a class scene when my partner said, "I've dropped my contact lens on the floor."

I blocked her offer and substituted my will for how the scene should unfold. "Oh no," I replied. "It's probably still in your eye. Let me look." I moved closer to have a look in her eye.

"No," she said angrily as she pushed me away. "I dropped it."

Even in a class during a theater game, I couldn't accept the reality my partner had described—that she dropped her contact lens. If I had made the obvious response and said, "Yikes! Contact on the floor! Don't move," my partner would have felt heard and validated, and an interesting scene might have evolved. Conflict happened instead, and the scene was over.

After coming face-to-face with my pattern of "no" saying that night, something inside me shifted. From that night forward, my vantage points and my perspectives were different. The healing impact of improvisation's moments ultimately affected every aspect of my life, including my community ministries and my personal and professional relationships.

My mother, Jeanne, was diagnosed with Alzheimer's in 2001— pre-improv. Both of her older sisters had died from Alzheimer's, so this diagnosis was not completely unexpected. Even so, the frightened, safety-seeking "no" sayer in me did my very best to avoid this reality—which wasn't too difficult, since I lived in Maine and Mom lived in Iowa.

In May 2003, however, I met Alzheimer's disease face-to-face when my cousin brought Mom to Maine for a visit "before it was too late," my cousin said, meaning before Mom forgot me (which she never did, by the way). During this short visit, I was deeply touched by my competent, independent mother's obvious decline and what I could only describe as her exquisite vulnerability. She seemed less guarded, more able to speak her truth, certainly more present in the moment. I shared with her that, in September, I would begin training for the ministry of spiritual direction, where I would learn to accompany spiritual seekers as they discovered a deeper relationship with themselves, others, and God.

Because she was angry and critical—"Devastated," she said—when she learned that I would be ordained as a Unitarian Universalist minister and no longer Catholic, I was not expecting support from her about my training to become a spiritual director. But she surprised me by expressing interest in this ministry. Over the next year, when we spoke on the phone, she always asked about spiritual direction. In one of her letters, she asked me if I could teach her to pray better. In another, she mentioned how kind I had been to her—she said she never realized that I was so caring. My heart was touched. Through her vision, sharpened by diminished cognition, it seemed my mother was seeing me for the first time.

During the summer of 2004, discoveries began happening that seemingly rewired everything for Mom and me, opening the doorway to my next community ministry. In June, my older sister, who was living with Mom, asked me to come to Iowa for two weeks so she could go on a camping vacation. Mom could no longer be left alone, and on their previous summer trip—which ended with the Minnesota State Police finding Mom on I-35, walking home to Dubuque, followed by a night in the hospital emergency room—my sister had learned that taking Mom camping was a bad idea. Because of the quality of the time I had with Mom in Maine, and the endearing letters and phone conversations we had shared since then, I was eager to spend more time with her, so I joyfully said yes to this request.

After hearing my yes, my sister went on to share some alarming details. "Mom is really uncooperative, angry, and combative. She won't eat, take her medicine, or do what I tell her to do. In order to get her to 'obey,' you'll have to raise your voice, threaten to take her to the mental hospital, or give her the antipsychotic drugs I got from her internist." She paused and added, "Those drugs do make her kind of out of it for weeks, though."

At this point, I became very worried, wondering, *What in the world have I said yes to?*

I later learned that my sister's approach is pretty common, even now. People who don't understand what's happening for those who experience cognitive decline get frustrated, and sometimes they yell, threaten, and use physical force or drugs trying to get people living with Alzheimer's and dementia under control. But taking this approach with my exquisitely vulnerable mother was completely unacceptable to me, and I was determined to find another way. I searched the internet for ideas about compassionate caregiving but didn't find any help, not even from the Alzheimer's Association website. Remember, it was 2004, and there wasn't much available then.

Days before leaving for Iowa, I spoke to my ministry mentor, Rev. Libbie Stoddard, who noticed my distress. She recommended a new book that had recently been published, *Learning to Speak Alzheimer's* by Joanne Koenig Coste. I ordered the book overnight express, and it arrived just in time for me to toss it into my carry-on bag.

While reading the book in the plane, I had a flash of an idea that trying improvisation with Mom—meeting her in her world, her reality, as all the experts were suggesting, and making her "look good"—might be a more compassionate, caring, and effective way to connect with her.

During those two weeks in Iowa, Mom gave me countless opportunities to practice saying yes to her surprising offers, just like in improv class. When I was able to meet her in her world, she wasn't the angry, combative person I was expecting.

During one such moment with Mom, we had planned an outing to the nursing home to visit Mom's "boyfriend," Merlin, and when it was nearly time to go, I asked Mom, "Are you ready?"

Visibly upset by my question, she replied, "We can't go."

I reacted with curiosity. "But I thought you wanted to see Merlin."

"Not now," Mom said. "This is the time that Milly comes to visit me."

Milly died in 1991; we had planted flowers on her grave the day before. Instead of correcting Mom and possibly demeaning her for forgetting or breaking her heart by reminding her that her beloved sister was long dead, I chose to improvise. I joined Mom in her world, where we were expecting Milly, and I said the next logical thing.

"Well, what would you think about leaving Milly a note, telling her where we are, and asking her to come in and wait for us?"

After pausing for a moment, Mom said, "That's a good idea."

"Okay," I said. "Could you get a piece of paper and a pencil, and we'll write the note?"

"Oh yes, I'll do that." And she was off to find the paper and pencil. I wrote the note, Mom taped it to the door, and we went to visit Merlin as planned.

Improvisers would call my response *accepting and advancing the offer*, also known as saying, "Yes, and . . ." Alzheimer's experts would identify this as a *therapeutic fiblet*. Spiritual teachers would call this accepting reality—Mom's reality, according to Alzheimer's—and would remind us that accepting reality in the present provides the most positive springboard into the future. In addition, scientific research has informed us that this kind of radical acceptance is one of the most effective coping techniques for relieving caregiver stress. Affirming this from the theological perspective, one of my important teachers, Jesuit Anthony DeMello, reminds us that the more we fight whatever "cloud" enters our lives, the more power we give it.

Through improvisation, Mom and I allowed her reality to spring us into a future that overflowed with connection and healing. The day before I was leaving to return to Maine, Mom was able to tell me that my efforts to learn about Alzheimer's, my attempts to communicate creatively by using improvisation, and my compassionate attention had made an impression on her. She looked up at me from her chair in the living room and said, "Will you stay and take care of me? You're kinder to me."

In reply, my heart shouted out, "Yes!" In that moment, my "yes"-saying adventure into my own personal healing through the Alzheimer's journey sprouted wings, and the seed was planted for my community ministry, Healing Moments for Alzheimer's, which would ultimately educate, inform, and inspire thousands of dementia caregivers.

While I was in Iowa with Mom, I interacted with the staff from the Alzheimer's Association, telling them about my discovery regarding Alzheimer's and improvisation. Fascinated, they suggested that I create a workshop about it. When I connected with the Massachusetts chapter about the idea, they were equally intrigued.

In his book, *Hearing God's Call: Ways of Discernment for Clergy and Laity*, Ben Campbell Johnson reminded me that God's call can be much broader and deeper than a call to lead a congregation, and that these divine calls are happening in our lives all the time. God beckons us into ordinary situations and bestows upon us an honor unequaled in human experience: the opportunity to share in the world's divine mission. "The call of God to a vocation," Johnson writes, "begins as an idea in your mind, often triggered by an event," such as the Alzheimer's diagnosis of a loved one, in my case. To receive God's call, Johnson recommends being silent and paying attention to our lives, including the affirmation of our ideas and invitations that come to us from others. It occurred to me that input from others about improvisation and Alzheimer's could be revealing my call to a unique community ministry. Guidance from my ministry mentor; discoveries in a book; encouragement from the Alzheimer's Associations in Iowa and Massachusetts, followed by enthusiastic feedback from a psychiatrist in Maine who was a director of multiple nursing homes in New England; and collaboration with a Boston improviser . . . they all seemed to be watering the seeds for my Healing Moments for Alzheimer's Ministry.

When I reflect about the evolution of my ministry for Alzheimer's, I recall a poster hanging in the waiting room of the career-counseling office where I had my psychological evaluation for ministry in 1990. While the poster featured a quote by Richard N. Bolles, the author of *What Color Is Your Parachute?*, the message I remember and carry with me encouraged me to humbly embrace my ministry because I am not alone in my work—ever. Although the inspiration for the Healing Moments for Alzheimer's Ministry arose from my own desire to care for my mother with kindness and compassion, I realized that my most inspired and inspiring creations, my most important accomplishments, have not and will not come about through my efforts alone. I and God—and quite often, authors, teachers, counselors, friends, colleagues, reporters, sometimes even enlightening television programs—are cocreators.

A year after my summer with Mom and the improvisation/ Alzheimer's seed planting, my two-year spiritual direction training program was ending. Since I wasn't ready to end my study of spirituality, I applied to the Doctor of Ministry program in Faith, Health, and Spirituality at Andover Newton Seminary. Once accepted, I moved back to Boston and started classes at ANTS and ImprovBoston "University." It seemed like an odd combination to others, but to me, it made perfect sense.

Thanks to the opportunities given to me by my advisor at ANTS, Dr. Brita Gill-Austern, professor of psychology and pastoral theology, this time period helped my two paths of ministry germinate. When Dr. Gill-Austern learned that I was developing an Alzheimer's improvisation program, she was excited about the innovative nature of the project, as well as the potential for healing in the face of an incurable disease. She and her program committee voted to provide me with a grant to fund the start-up costs of the ministry. She then invited me to make a presentation for her pastoral care and counseling class for the section on aging, which was so well-received that she asked me to develop a daylong workshop for students and the surrounding community. The workshop, "Meet in the Moment: Saying 'Yes' to Alzheimer's," was offered at the Andover Newton campus on October 27, 2007.

Dr. Gill-Austern also encouraged and supported me in my desire to develop and offer spiritual direction groups for seminarians, bringing to them what I lacked and longed for in my seminary training. I loved this group work, as well as my individual spiritual direction practice, and was sure that this and teaching courses on spirituality would be my forever career.

Then the beckoning that Ben Campbell Johnson wrote about happened to me again. In fall 2006, my sister moved Mom into a nursing home. Six months later, my sister relocated to New Mexico. There was my mother, living with Alzheimer's disease, alone in a care center in Dubuque, Iowa—1200 miles away from both of her daughters. I was in turmoil about her life situation. After almost a year of discernment, I moved to Iowa in February 2008, grateful that ANTS would allow me to complete my degree via online courses and independent study and heartsick to think that I was abandoning my spiritual direction work.

It turned out not to be a forever abandonment, since spiritual direction is and always will be my foundational ministry; it shines a light over everything I do. While it looked as if my ministry changed from spiritual direction to educating Alzheimer's caregivers when I moved to Iowa, it didn't change; it expanded. My ministries of Healing Moments for Alzheimer's and spiritual direction merged.

I walked through the doors of Stonehill Care Center with the fresh eyes of a spiritual director looking for God—in all the wrong places, some would declare. If history were the only predictor, it surely seemed as if it would be the wrong place for me to find God. (When I was in my early thirties and back in Iowa visiting Mom, she took me to the nursing home to visit her sister, Milly. Seeing Milly's vacant eyes and the restraints holding her upright in her wheelchair—no longer a legal intervention—and the baby doll she clutched in her lap caused me to flee from the nursing home. Sobbing, I waited for Mom in the car, and for once, she didn't criticize me. It seemed she understood, and she never asked me to go again.) Benedictine monk Brother David Steindl-Rast defines God as "surprise" and hope as "being open to surprise." Finding myself wanting and willing to be with Mom in her current "home" was definitely a surprise.

By some stroke of good luck, the first semester I was in Iowa, ANTS offered an online class called "Ministry to the Elderly." I signed up immediately, thinking it might help me—and it did, for in that class and all my subsequent classes, I wrote papers about spirituality and Alzheimer's, recognizing the inherent worth and dignity of the cognitively impaired and delving deeply into the spirituality of caregiving. My research intertwined with my caring for Mom and all of her neighbors with dementia, as well as with my meetings with other caregivers in Iowa and around the country, including Unitarian Universalist minister Rev. Dr. Carl Scovel, who had shared with me that caring for his mother, Myra, who had Alzheimer's, led to a transformation in his life, ministry, relationship to God, and prayer.

After reading a few of my papers, Dr. Gill-Austern remarked that I didn't seem to be suffering. She was curious about this, since other dementia caregivers she knew reported terrible suffering. My initial reaction was to wonder if I was doing something wrong.

But I couldn't deny the truth of my own experience. One night, as I was walking over to see Mom, I noticed a lightness in my steps; I was eager and enthusiastic on my mission to spend time with her. As I arrived at the door of the care center, I literally felt joyful. *Whoa,* I thought. *This isn't the typical reaction of people visiting loved ones in nursing homes or care centers or dementia units.*

It took some reflection for me to be able to understand this surprising feeling. One important realization was that I didn't get to joy by denying the realities of Alzheimer's, which, as everyone knows, involves diminishments, losses, challenges, hardships, sadness, and powerlessness ... to begin the list. I got to joy by embracing all of these realities, feeling my feelings, drying my tears, and then seeing what else I could see.

My vision was enhanced by the following poem by Rev. Dr. Carl Scovel's mother.

The Wind of The Spirit by Myra Scovel

Where does the wind come from, Nicodemus?
Rabbi, I do not know.
Nor can you tell where it will go.

Put yourself into the path of the wind, Nicodemus.
You will be borne along
by something greater than yourself.
You are proud of your position,
content in your security,
but you will perish in such stagnant air.

Put yourself into the path of the wind, Nicodemus.
Bright leaves will dance before you.
You will find yourself in places
you never dreamed of going;
you will be forced into situations
you have dreaded
and find them like a coming home.

You will have a power you never had before, Nicodemus.
You will be a new man.

Put yourself into the path of the wind.

What I saw in that care center was truly like bright leaves danc-
ing before me. Through my eyes looking for God, I was able to see
clearly that people with Alzheimer's and other dementias still have so
much potential. If we let them, they have the potential to inspire us,
teach us, love us, heal us, amuse us, befriend us, calm us, touch us,
energize us, enlighten us, empower us, forgive us, nurture us, open
our hearts, bring out the best in us, and bring meaning and purpose
into our lives—and yes, bring us moments of amazement and joy.

We may be surprised to realize that people with Alzheimer's
still have the capacity to show us how to be humble and trusting and
courageous and receptive, how to be authentically ourselves in this

present moment. We may be surprised to discover that when we look beneath memory loss and the inability to reason or to care for themselves, people with Alzheimer's can and do reveal to us the inherent worth and dignity of every person, as well as the true value of life—theirs *and* ours. In their ever-remaining ability to freely give and receive love, they show us what it really means to be human.

I thought that coming to Iowa to care for my mother would be a sacrifice, but the choice, experience, and years following her death led to a powerful transformation in my ministry and personal life. The Healing Moments for Alzheimer's Ministry, which has offered a variety of programming all around the country, has grown from a single workshop into multiple formats, including workshops and conference presentations designed specifically for congregations, family caregivers, and medical and care center staff. The papers I wrote for ANTS went various creative directions; one paper became an educational play titled *The Forgiving and The Forgetting: Hope and Healing for Alzheimer's*, designed for a multidisciplinary audience of family and professional caregivers that creatively and compassionately unites dramatic storytelling, spirituality, improvisation, and Alzheimer's science. It was performed live at an Alzheimer's Association conference in Dubuque, Iowa, as well as at conferences on spirituality and aging in Chicago and Los Angeles (an audio recording of the play has been produced and is now available on YouTube). Excerpts of other papers became the sermons for worship and healing services and have been offered at UU churches around the country. (They are recorded on the CD *Meeting Alzheimer's: Companionship on the Journey—A Heartfelt Introduction to Alzheimer's Disease.*)

All the papers were eventually combined in my book published by Skinner House, *Where Two Worlds Touch: A Spiritual Journey Through Alzheimer's Disease*. One reviewer, Patty Sutherland of *Foreword Reviews*, described the book as "consciousness-raising and world view-shifting," suggesting that the "insights found in *Where Two Worlds Touch* might have a positive systemic impact on society if it were to become the go-to book for those whose lives are touched by Alzheimer's." I'm proud and honored to say that the book is a real-life representation of the healing principles of Unitarian Universalism theology put into practice.

In 2014, I cocreated a research protocol of my workshop for family caregivers—"Meeting Alzheimer's: Learning to Communicate and Connect"—with the University of Iowa Department of Neurology. The study results showed that after attending my workshop, Alzheimer's and dementia family caregivers experienced a significant reduction in their stress, an increase in their feelings of confidence and competence in their role as caregivers, and improved quality of life for their loved ones and themselves. The results were published in 2018 in *Alzheimer's & Dementia: Translational Research & Clinical Interventions*.

The breadth and depth of the Healing Moments for Alzheimer's Ministry is reflective of my own process of wrestling with an unknown; learning from spiritual authors, Alzheimer's experts, and other caregivers; and then documenting what I noticed about myself, my mother, others, Alzheimer's, and God. But because I am not a minister working in a church and many of my workshops are not overtly spiritual, people often ask me, "Why is this ministry and not social work or counseling, or purely caregiver education?"

In addition to following the beckoning of the Spirit that invited me onto this path, I believe the work is ministry because it opens a door to healing for others. I believe that our individual lived experiences tap into universal truths about human challenges and woundedness. If I have this question, this sorrow, this wound, this challenge, it's likely that others do as well. My work offers the potential for significant personal and spiritual transformation for caregivers.

A few months after Mom died, I collaborated with a group of people to create the *Meeting Alzheimer's* album. One of the songs, "I Open My Heart," was written specifically for this resource. When we had a proof copy ready for review, I went to the songwriter's house so we could listen together. As I was leaving, she said to me, "You're a most unique combination of qualities. You're both really organized and really sweet."

I paused for a minute, taking this in, and replied with what was true for me. "I used to just be organized. Caring for my mom made me sweet."

I'm still very organized, but now, having experienced a whole different world with Mom and others with dementia, my preferred way of being is sweet, and kind, and present in the moment.

Dr. Stephen G. Post, author of *The Moral Challenge of Alzheimer Disease* and *Dignity for Deeply Forgetful People: How Caregivers Can Meet the Challenges of Alzheimer's Disease,* bases his dementia-care recommendations on the importance of being kind rather than right. He was and is a profound teacher and mentor for me on this journey; he actually predicted my transformation when he wrote, "The person with Alzheimer's is eventually swept away, while caregivers look back and feel forever changed by their experiences."

In the introduction to *Dignity for Deeply Forgetful People,* Dr. Post acknowledges that he writes to transform cultural attitudes about people with Alzheimer's and dementia, whom he refers to as "the deeply forgetful," a phrase he believes will help dismantle the wall of separation between us and them. I am so honored that Dr. Post, recognizing the resonance of our work, is including in his book a lengthy description of my workshop, "Meeting Alzheimer's: Learning to Communicate and Connect," which he describes as a "caregiver resilience program." In many ways, the workshop is a practical expression of the inspiration I received from him when I began the journey; I feel great joy and gratitude that a flash of inspiration in an airplane somewhere over Michigan has manifested into a ministry that is helping to support and bring hope and healing to deeply forgetful people and those who love and care for them.

My mother died from Alzheimer's in 2011. Caring for her was and remains the most important and most transforming ministry of my life. The situation I had consciously dreaded—the responsibility of caring for my alcoholic, abandoning, abusive mother—became a coming-home of sorts, just as Myra Scovel predicted it would be if I put myself in the path of the wind. Although I may not yet be "perfectly okay not knowing what the %@#%! is going on," as my diploma from ImprovBoston proclaims me to be, this recovering "no" sayer is now more curious than afraid of what is yet to be revealed as I journey on, listening and paying attention to the beckoning of the Spirit in all of its glorious forms.

Where Unity Lies, Wholeness Within

Rev. Dr. Azande Sasa

As a Unitarian Universalist military chaplain, I often find myself reflecting on the following questions: How do we integrate who we once were into who we are? How do we create wholeness within? How do we reconcile the seeming contradictions with which we live every day?

In my final year of divinity school, the prospective graduates gathered in a circle to share what we planned to do after graduation. One of my fellow students announced that she was going to be a military chaplain. My immediate thought was, *Why on earth would someone want to do that?* I often come back to that initial feeling of dismay and wonder where it came from.

Did it come from my mother, who was more than slightly disappointed to find that her on-scholarship, private school–educated daughter, whom she had worked two jobs to raise, had joined the military? Did it come from my own internalized sexism, which had

Rev. Dr. Azande Sasa (she/her) is a former Arabic linguist and an ordained community minister with the Unitarian Universalist Association. She served as a military chaplain at her previous assignment in Clarksville, Tennessee. Azande is the author of the upcoming book *Interlife: Near Death Consciousness as the Key to Profound Living* under the name Azande Mangeango.

impressed upon me that the military was not for women? Did it come from my irrational, poor person's elitism that compelled me to believe that the military is not a profession for the highly educated? Did it come from my then-burgeoning Afrocentrism, fostered by my desire to reconstruct my own South Sudanese, African American identity, that interrogated all things patriotic—American, even? Did it come from my deeply spiritual roots that found me averse to the idea of harming another being? Or, in a much more innocuous vein, did my initial response simply bespeak my ignorance?

To this day, I laugh at myself. I had no idea that I would one day turn out to be in the Armed Forces. Quite frankly, the military had not entered my realm of possibilities. I never *decided* to be a military chaplain. Instinctively, as if stepping into my life's path, military chaplaincy decided on me.

Now, in hindsight, there is no place I would rather do ministry.

It took more than a decade for me to transform my initial dismay at the notion of military chaplaincy into pride to don the uniform. My route was circuitous and, at times, unnecessarily painful. But if retelling my story can prevent anyone else an ounce of pain—by helping others get greater clarity about their own calling, perhaps—then it is well worth it.

After graduating from Harvard Divinity School in 2000, I was quite content to work in urban, immigration, and community ministerial positions. Yet within a few short years, I was laid off due to budget cuts and found myself at one of those proverbial "now what?" life moments.

I decided to take a detour back to school in the form of a PhD in sociocultural anthropology at the University of Chicago, with a specialization in indigenous religions in South Sudan. Here's where the story takes a strange twist: On the way to the University of Chicago, I passed a military recruiter's office twice a day, every day. The seed was planted. Six arduous years later, after completing all of my coursework and field research, the stirrings of my call to ministry quickened once again.

One day, after reaching my saturation point with a program that could have easily stretched on another few years, I found myself in the recruiter's office. It could have been any branch of service, for all I knew, but I chose the Army. In hindsight, I believe my decision derived from an accumulation of daily trips past the recruiter's office and the subliminal messaging from all of those "be all that you can be" commercials. Whatever the reason, there I found myself.

"Can I help you?" the recruiter asked.

"I want to be a chaplain," I said, much to my own surprise.

That was where things went sour. Please take note: If you want to be a military chaplain, talk to another chaplain, talk to a chaplain recruiter, talk to the Unitarian Universalist Association, but please, don't just walk into a recruiter's office.

She informed me that I had to enlist before becoming a chaplain—which was not true. When looking over possible jobs, she offered me a chaplain assistant position. Somehow, I had the presence of mind to turn this down; it didn't seem right to be a chaplain assistant when I was already an ordained minister.

"What other jobs do you have?"

"How about a linguist?"

Bingo! I'd loved languages all my life.

When I arrived at basic training in Fort Leonard Wood, Missouri, the sergeant major noticed my educational background and experience and inquired, "What are you doing here?"

"My recruiter told me I had to enlist first." I replied.

The senior noncommissioned officers burst into laughter. Booksmart but military-naive, it took three years before I could switch over to the Chaplain Corps, three years that were filled with the challenges of serving as a junior-enlisted soldier at nearly twice the age and experience level of my peers. That being said, I do not regret a minute of my detour. I learned a beautiful language, which I still maintain, and most importantly, I walked directly in the shoes of many of the soldiers I now serve.

I will never forget my last day as Specialist (SPC) Sasa. A soldier did something to tick off the sergeant major. As a result, at 2000 hours (8:00 p.m.), on a dark Friday night, there we were on all fours, picking weeds by hand. All I could do was laugh; the next day, I would be driving to Fort Jackson, South Carolina, to the US Army Chaplain Center and School (USACHCS) to take the Oath of Commissioned Officers to become a chaplain. To serve is to empathize and know the path that those you are serving have tread.

Pivotal moments, figures, and faith influences were instrumental in my transformation to Chaplain Sasa. As I mentioned, I took an unusually long hiatus away from ministry to pursue my doctoral studies, so I was unsure if I would even be endorsed by the UUA due to my inactive status. But if not for the support of our beloved UU faith community, I would not be here today. They believed in me when I did not believe in myself. They refused to give up on me.

Among these faith angels is Sarah Lammert, the UU endorser for all branches of service. When I called her out of the clear blue to say, *I want to be a UU military chaplain*—a germ of a dream, three years in incubation—not only did she not shut the door as I had feared but she also opened the door and guided me to the other side.

Through that door of UU military chaplaincy, I found a family of supportive peers, fellow chaplains representing all branches. Sarah informed me that she would be hosting the first gathering of UU military chaplains; she was gracious enough to invite me to attend. I did and have not missed an annual gathering since. I affectionately refer to it as our pilgrimage because it is one of the few sanctuaries where we UU military chaplains are free to be ourselves, to share our joys and pains, and to hold one another in our diverse and meaningful ministries. Throughout those precious few days, we nurture and sustain one another. This group has been integral to my ability to thrive as a low-density (minority faith) UU chaplain in the military.

Part of my path back to ministry involved establishing a strong connection with a UU church. I chose the First Unitarian Universalist Church of Nashville (FUUN), whose senior minister, Rev. Gail S. Seavey, was another faith angel. FUUN was nearly one and a half hours from my base and the largest UU church in the vicinity; it took me a few Sundays to garner the strength to come out to the congregation as a soldier. From my formative years in the seminary, I recalled a UU environment inhospitable to the notion of the military and, by extension, military service.

Once I came forward about the truth of who I was—a soldier—the floodgates opened. It turns out there was no shortage of former service members who were waiting to recount their experiences during previous wars. I will never forget the relief on the face of a former Vietnam Army nurse when she held my hands, looked me in the eye, and thanked me; I knew that I had tapped into something profound and unexpressed. The overwhelming response at the Nashville parish did not reflect my experience as a Unitarian Universalist in our epicenter, Boston, a decade ago. What was different? Was it my geographical location, Nashville? (The music was certainly much better!) Was it a sea change? Or had my perceptions been overblown?

There was a time when I believed my Ancestors would not have approved of my status as a military member. Perhaps I did not give them enough credit. When I say *Ancestors*, I am referring to the two types, family and faith—blood kin and those with whom we feel a kindred spirit. These are the Ancestors who have gone before us and opened the road, so to speak. They are our Ancestors in calling, souls with whom we feel connected, with whom we feel a quickening while hearing their words or ideas. They may be faith Ancestors, such as Emerson or Channing; philosophical Ancestors, such as the Founding Mothers and Fathers; social justice Ancestors, such as Mahatma Gandhi or Nelson Mandela; or inventive Ancestors, such as Nikola Tesla or Albert Einstein. Whoever they are, there is an indescribable *something* about that person in whose footsteps we tread that inspires us. Shortly after leaving the ministry and gaining some clarity on the future direction of his life as a lecturer, Ralph Waldo Emerson said, "The call of our calling is the loudest call." Sometimes we have to leave to come to ourselves.

I joined the military when the Don't Ask, Don't Tell policy was still in effect. I brought a UU lens to my chaplaincy, refusing to allow artificial, human-made barriers of gender, sexual orientation, or ethnicity stand in the way of love. While Unitarian Universalists are not known for evangelism, our mere presence in an environment like the military makes us agents of change.

As a Unitarian Universalist who fully embraces the First Principle, which affirms the inherent worth and dignity of all beings, I found it difficult to accept the military's hierarchical structure as a means to mete out respect. After an incident where a fellow soldier was quick to ascertain my rank before responding to a polite, "Excuse me," I vowed not to be one of those people who looked at someone's chest, where rank insignia is worn, before determining how to address a fellow being. That was ten years ago. I have since outlived my youthful indignation and come to see the utility in knowing where one stands in the rank structure in order to interact appropriately.

There were many other opportunities for growth along the way. My first assignment was Fort Drum, New York. Note: With life in general, and especially with the military, be very specific about what you desire. I requested a vague, "something on the East Coast, near a big city like New York." I was sent to Fort Drum, home of the other New York, known for record snowfalls from October to June and nearly a two-hour drive from the closest city.

As the newly minted Chaplain Sasa, I was one of a few female chaplains assigned to an all-male brigade combat team (BCT) of approximately seven hundred soldiers. Prior to reporting to my unit, my astute supervisory chaplain tried to prepare me for the battlefield by informing me that I would be one of a handful of women in an all-male BCT. Fortunately for me, I did not know what that meant; as it was my first assignment, there was no precedent. Ignorance, in that instance, was bliss.

Despite my own lack of awareness, my career in the military has been checkered by great mentors like my former supervisor, who cared along the way, and a nurturing Chaplain Corps. I am grateful to have received some of the most fantastic assignments; even the difficult experiences have been a blessing. Opposition can be our best friend.

The military is miles ahead of most of society in terms of respecting and honoring diversity, which makes me extremely proud to be part of such an organization. Gender pay disparity, for example, which is widespread in the civilian sector, is not as prevalent in the military, where pay is based on rank. But there are pockets in the military similar to nested dolls, and one of those pockets is a Corps. In the Corps, there are chaplains representing denominations that have their own cultural and theological composition. It's fascinating to witness how these microcosms blend and what emerges out of these social admixtures.

When I arrived at Fort Drum, a senior chaplain pulled me aside and handed me a printout from the internet on Unitarian Universalism and told me that I would not be participating in worship on his post. At the time, I did not realize that he was not acting on behalf of the Corps—he was acting on behalf of his own faith dictates.

I was woefully unprepared for the challenge of working with other faith groups in a worship setting. I saw with rose-colored UU glasses, believing that we are all siblings in faith. We Unitarian Universalists dwell in a world where pagans, Buddhists, Humanists, Wiccans, Christians, atheists, deists, and nearly every faith under the sun sit side-by-side on any given Sunday. We should not expect such willing comingling among all our peers. There are some chaplains who cannot, due to the dictates of their faith, lead worship with a woman or someone from a different theological background, such as Unitarian Universalism.

It is essential to err on the side of respecting and honoring another chaplain's faith. We clergy members are in the military to accommodate soldiers' rights to the free practice of religion and, at times, we are called upon to accommodate other chaplains' rights as well. We serve in a religious capacity in a diverse faith environment; that is what we signed up for. Experiences will be thick (in the Geertzian sense), juicy, and never boring.

Early challenges aside, there has never been a better time to serve in the Chaplain Corps, given its refreshing emphasis on embracing and nurturing the capacity of each soldier as an intrinsically spiritual being.

The military is a great testing ground. You will always be challenged to stretch, grow, and see things from far outside of your comfort zone. A growing majority of soldiers describe themselves as "spiritual but not religious" or as having "no religious preference"— affectionately known as the "nones" or "dones" (as in, done with religion). But when soldiers come to you for support or counseling, perhaps due to marital issues, a painful moral injury, or posttraumatic stress, they're not asking, *What's your faith background, chaplain?* Nine times out of ten, they do not care. They simply want someone to share their burden, hear their story, and accompany them in the most desperate of times.

My second assignment was as a cemetery chaplain at Arlington National Cemetery (ANC)—the assignment of a lifetime. Funerary military chaplaincy appeals to me because it entails accompanying families through a time of great poignancy. The officiating chaplain becomes the face of the military for families at their most critical times of need. It is a privilege to be with them as they say goodbye to their loved one and watch them part with a sense of peace, knowing they honored their beloved with dignity. Arlington is, in so many ways, a place of healing.

Decades ago, prior to my military service, I felt as if I didn't fit into the social fabric of America. The transformation may have occurred gradually, but I didn't notice until I was assigned to the cemetery. In the cemetery, part of me died and part of me came to life.

In my case, patriotism was not something I was born or raised with; it was something I had to learn. At Arlington, I learned patriotism. Before it was known as Arlington National Cemetery, the lands on which the cemetery rests once belonged to George Washington Parke Custis, grandson of Martha Washington and stepgrandson of George Washington. Custis built Arlington House as a memorial to his grandfather and the nation's first president. During the Civil War, the grounds became a refuge for formerly enslaved Africans escaping the South in search of a better life. The refuge grew into a bustling community with a robust infrastructure to include a school, a hospital, a home for the elderly, and other public services. Given the high number of casualties, the Army decided to use the land as a burial ground shortly after the Civil War. Many of the freed Africans left, but according to the records, nearly four thousand remained and maintained the land. That was their home. They are, to this day, the few civilians other than military dependents buried at ANC, primarily in section 27. Their grave markers are sparse, for the most part, with the simple inscription, CITIZEN, or CIVILIAN, in some cases. One of the most notable citizens is Selina Gray, a personal maid of Mrs. Robert E. Lee (née Mary Custis), the only child of George Washington Parke Custis. Ms. Gray kept the Arlington Estate when the Lee family evacuated in 1861. Without these enslaved Africans, what we know as Arlington House and a great deal of the Washington family history may not have survived. Their quarters and the Lee House remain to this day there for all to see. I spent hours visiting those rooms and imagining life from their perspective.

People often ask about the most memorable funeral I've ever done. There are so many, but one that stands out in the top few was a service I conducted for the descendants of a prominent Confederate warrior. I will not say who, out of respect for the family, but when I saw the name, I knew.

Had I sensed that my presence was a hindrance to the family, I would have happily excused myself as I had done in the case of another service, where the grieving son was a born-again Christian and opposed to the idea of a woman conducting his father's service. The chaplain is only the conduit, the vehicle—never an impediment. Ministry, especially funerary ministry, is the ultimate expression of empathy, and empathy and indignation are two vessels that cannot be held with the same hand. Being in the cemetery forced me to exercise my "moral imagination," to borrow a term from Rev. Nathan C. Walker, who wrote *Cultivating Empathy: The Worth and Dignity of Every Person—Without Exception*. Exercising the moral imagination, according to Walker, is an "everyday spiritual practice" which we enact as a "proven remedy for otherizing." Understanding, Walker reminds us, does not mean agreement. However, if we perhaps set about this arduous practice by suspending our preconceived notions, if only for a moment; transcending our self-imposed lines of demarcation, if only for a moment; and entertaining the thought of life from another perspective, all hatred would cease. Prior to my cemetery chaplaincy, I thought I had it all figured out. In the cemetery, I realized how little I really knew. I know nothing. I found a new appreciation of Paul's pronouncement, "I die daily" (1 Corinthians 15:31).

I was relieved that when I entered the family room to meet them, they did not do a double take. They did not even blink an eye. Of course, I treated them with the utmost care and compassion, as I did every grieving family. They could not have been more gracious. I mentioned their Ancestor in the service, and I was honored to lift up his name because it created meaning for them.

My time in Arlington National Cemetery was like water being poured upon the salt of my experience, washing away sedimented cynicism I may have had toward the history of this country. The lens through which I saw this nation expanded, and I embraced what it means to be American. I've always been a child of God, and I will always be. I will always have a soul that is eternal, not limited to any label or identity, but I needed to walk in that identity to respect the totality of who I am. As we tread on the interstices of identity, we often feel as if we have to be one, the other, both, or none at all. Growing up in a sociocultural no-man's-land, neither this nor that but too much of either, I took for granted my American identity. In my youthful, idealistic mind, Mother Africa needed me more. Yet walking through the hallowed, silent markers of sacrifice, I could feel the presence of stories. The stones did not lie. They told the history of a nation whose divided, troubled past could be overcome. Death is the great common denominator and the overarching unifier. In the cemetery, privates rested beside generals, presidents in the company of enslaved Africans and their descendants. I could hear them—all of them. *Listen*, they said through the hush of the unspoken word, beckoning me to hear with my inner being. I realized by serving alongside the people who bled for this country, who died for this country, who sacrificed their life force for this country, I was serving Africa. In the interconnectedness of all things, good is good, service is service. Are there any distinctions when one serves to make the world a better place?

The above is the spirit and the call of military chaplaincy, a form of community ministry. The following are the nuts and bolts.

While each branch of service has its idiosyncrasies, no matter which branch one chooses, the primary purpose of a military chaplain is to ensure their soldiers' rights to the free practice of religion. They are there to make sure that their commander is complying with Title 10 of the US Code and that the commander's personnel are able to practice their faith, mission allowing. How does this awesome task manifest on the ground? A chaplain, for example, may have to advocate for a soldier to switch shifts with someone else so that they may observe their holy day, or a chaplain may be called upon to write a memo for a soldier so that they may receive their meal allowance in order to practice the dietary dictates of their faith.

Chaplains are assigned an enlisted soldier, known as a religious affairs specialist, who provides the pulse of the enlisted side. When deployed, the chaplain does not carry a weapon. They do not fight. They are noncombatants. The chaplain and the religious affairs specialist are the only personnel in the military who have 100 percent confidentiality, which allows soldiers to feel safe when they seek counseling. Military chaplains conduct a great deal of counseling, so it is important to be intentional about strengthening one's counseling skills.

The Army considers chaplains to be soldiers first. If the unit goes to the field, the chaplain goes with them. If the unit conducts a rotation or deploys, the chaplain goes with them. Military chaplains do what their soldiers do, and go where their soldiers go.

Chaplains often face others' perceptions of them. Everyone has a preconceived notion of who and what a chaplain is, whether it is Father Mulcahy from *M*A*S*H* or the soapbox preacher from the neighborhood. I can't tell you how many times I've heard, "Don't swear around the chaplain!" as if chaplains have never sworn in their lives. Chaplains should be aware when entering a unit that they are walking into other people's impressions of who and what they are—good, bad, and ugly—which is perhaps no different from any other ministry. What matters is that among these perceptions, the chaplain remains theologically grounded and steadfast in their love and support for those whom they serve.

It should go without saying, but the military is not a place to proselytize. There is still a gray area around evangelizing; it is allowed in the context of counseling, if one seeks or asks for faith guidance. However, proselytization is against Army regulations. A military chaplain's sole purpose is to ensure their soldiers' rights to the free practice of religion. There is nothing more rewarding than knowing that one's primary reason for being there is to make sure that service members have the opportunity to practice their faith. In that sense, chaplains could be considered spiritual midwives. They directly tend to the soul, spiritual fitness, and morale of a group of dedicated people who have sworn their lives in service to the nation.

When one joins the military, they belong to the military. They have to be willing to put their health and life on the line because they will be called upon to go to dangerous places and do dangerous things. If they want to be a military chaplain, they have to take good care of themselves. It's awesome to be in a vocation that deems working out to be an integral part of one's job. As such, chaplains have an opportunity to undergo cool trainings like Airborne, Air Assault, or Ranger School. The sky is wide open, based on what chaplains are willing to invest.

Professional development is key. The chaplain must take any opportunity they can for refresher courses in counseling, preaching, or other pertinent skills. It is the chaplain's responsibility to stay emotionally and spiritually fit so that they can be the best that they can be for their people. When service members seek guidance, they do not want to find the chaplain crumbling under the weight of their own crisis or falling asleep during a counseling session because they are not sleeping well. Chaplains who are purposeful about their self-care are best able to represent God's goodness and wholeness to their soldiers.

Every day, every week, every year varies as a military chaplain. Yes, there is the mundane routine—Monday morning formations, routine staff meetings, PowerPoint presentations (the military loves PowerPoint). Interwoven with the mundane is the spectacularly present moment. One never knows when the life-or-death situation will be waiting at the office, the smoke pit, or the motor pool. Military chaplains become very comfortable with the notion of *ministry of presence* but have to reformulate what that presence means in their ever-changing world. On some occasions, presence can mean running "dog hill" for physical training; assisting soldiers in conducting preventive maintenance checks and service on their vehicles at the motor pool on Mondays; or showing up at 4:30 in the morning to go to the shooting range. Whatever the situation, military chaplains must get accustomed to the notion of change. They move frequently if they are active duty. They call parts of the world home that they never knew existed. If the chaplain has a family, they will experience the world along with the chaplain. When the chaplain deploys, the family will be expected to carry on in their service member's absence.

Chaplains have a dual role as a staff officer and as a minister in a unit. Starting out, the unit or parish will more than likely be a battalion, which could range in size from one hundred and fifty to several hundred personnel and could include Department of Defense civilians. This may be confusing, but they will have several supervisors and two chains of command. First and foremost, the chaplain works for their commander; it is their responsibility to advise the command on all things pertaining to religion, morale, morals, ethics, and overall well-being of the unit. The chaplain may also engage in external advising concerning the role of religion in the unit's area of operations.

While the chaplain works for their commander, they must still abide by their chaplain chain's guidance. To that end, they will be expected to assist the garrison or installation chaplain's office, as well through participating in worship, events such as the annual National Day of Prayer, Easter Sunrise Services, and more.

As a UU military chaplain who was once afraid to identify myself as a member of the Armed Forces to my Nashville congregation, there is so much now that makes me proud. I am proud that the very first recognized chaplain of the Army on April 19, 1775, was the Rev. William Emerson, grandfather of Ralph Waldo Emerson. Later, the same year, Emerson was followed closely by the Rev. John Murray, a Universalist, the founder of American Universalism. Then-General George Washington issued the following order regarding Murray's appointment: *The Revd Mr John Murray is appointed Chaplain to the Rhode-Island Regiments and is to be respected as such.*

Why did Washington feel the need to issue an order with reference to this particular appointment? John Murray's appointment was met with much consternation on the part of Congregationalist, Presbyterian, and Anglican clergy, who also served as chaplains. They questioned the wisdom of General Washington putting a Universalist in charge of the care of the Rhode Island troops' souls. Washington immediately put all doubts to rest.

I had no idea when I made my full transition into the military chaplaincy as a Unitarian Universalist Army chaplain that I was following in the path of some of our very own faith Ancestors, such as the first female military chaplain, Ella Elvira Hobart Gibson. Ella served during the Civil War for the 1st Wisconsin Heavy Artillery regiment and was only posthumously promoted to captain by the former President George W. Bush in 2002. While Chaplain Ella was not a Unitarian Universalist, she was one of our closest faith cousins, a Spiritualist. Raised a devoted Christian, Ella grew restless in her faith and began to question it. She wanted more. She found truth in the social activism of her day—the suffragist movement, abolitionism, and her own brand of intuitional poetry. Yes, Chaplain Captain Ella Elvira Hobart Gibson certainly paved the way for where our feet have trod. She is one of many Ancestors.

There was a time when I believed my presence in these two seemingly parallel worlds, Unitarian Universalism and the military, was irretrievably irreconcilable. Given enough time, worlds that don't collide coalesce. It is gratifying to learn the extent of the entwinement between these seemingly disparate realms. May we all experience the wholeness of claiming and embracing the totality of who we are.

Q&A with
Rev. Marisol Caballero

For those who don't know much about the UUA or how it works, could you describe your job and what that kind of institutional ministry is like?

My title is Faith Innovation Specialist, and my office is called Office of Lifespan Faith Engagement. That is a merger between what used to be the Faith Development Office and the Youth and Young Adult Office. There's about twelve of us. I've been in this position since 2017.

I help good ideas come true with regard to faith development for all ages. My constituency is mostly religious educators but sometimes nonprofessionals as well; sometimes it's clergy themselves. Mostly, I help create and curate resources, and I also help connect people who are doing similar types of innovative work.

Innovative doesn't always mean brand-spanking-new. It could mean new to the congregation, new to the ministry. It's like, *Here's a problem—how are we going to solve it?* A couple times a month, I have open shop talk over Zoom, where anyone can come and problem-solve and ask questions. It's the most casual shop talk space

Rev. Marisol Caballero (she/her) is a faith innovation specialist in the UUA's Office of Lifespan Faith Engagement. She is currently serving DRUUMM, a Unitarian Universalist people of color organization, as coordinator of the Global Majorities Collective: a UU POC Project.

for religious educators of all stripes. If you're a minister, like me, who considers themselves a religious educator, it's for you. We talk about trends or problems. It's still a fairly new position, and I'm still swimming upstream in terms of getting people to know what I do.

For the next several years, the big thing that will probably inform the direction of my work is the Commission on Institutional Change's report. I did some of the writing and editing for the Study/Action Guide that's online for congregations. I do a lot of cross-department and cross-organization collaboration. I worked with the organizing teams from Side with Love to do the Thirty Days of Love activities thing. That's a ton of fun. That's one of my favorite things to do.

The report calls for OWL-like* antiracism curriculum. We interpret that as lifespan antiracism curriculum. We're working on an online curriculum where you click on tiles based on themes—for example, a topic like making friends—and there will be multimedia like YouTube videos, songs, and stories. Some are commissioned and created by UUs, some not. Every lesson will have the same format: Here's circle time, here's an art project, here's a video to watch, here's an activity. You can pop around. That's going to be ongoing. And since it's online, we're not going to wait until a whole series is finished to start putting them up, whereas with written curriculum, you'd have to get it all done before you publish.

When you're talking about antiracism and critical race theory, it's changing so fast and the language changes. You know better, you do better. It's like Jenga pieces; you can take out and put in as you go. I'm like a project manager or developmental editor, working across departments, talking with the Fahs Collaboration at Meadville, LREDA and UUMA, DRUUMM, checking in with BLUU.

---

* Editor's note: Our Whole Lives is a sexuality education curriculum for people of all ages, ranging from kindergarteners to older adults.

What makes this kind of ministry a good fit for you?

I bring a different perspective to the work. One of my big soapboxes—it will be on my gravestone—is "Who is the *we* here?" I will interrupt meetings, like, "*We* who? Are you talking to the whole staff or are you talking to white staff?"

I'm more of an idea person than a completing-projects person [laughs]. I'm really good at throwing ideas out there and seeing what sticks; that's why I'm a good person to noodle with when someone has a dilemma or possible solution. I also know lots of people, so I can connect people who are doing similar things.

Another important soapbox for me is that we don't have to compete for intellectual property or accolades—we could just work together to do the thing. That's a big shift. Staff changed with each [UUA] president; it was very "if you want to keep your job [when there's a leadership transition], you have to get your name on this." We all work together now. I reiterate that internally and externally, and I emphasize it as much as I can. The more I talk about it, I feel like the more it will come true.

How do you see the role of community ministry in the whole of Unitarian Universalism?

It's vital that community ministers have more recognition and respect than they get. I think it's an exploitative relationship between community ministers and congregations. They get the connection and bragging rights of the ministers' work in the greater community, sometimes without the minister getting any recognition. The people in the pews may know nothing about the community minister, but publicly, the church gets seen. I think the work that community ministers do is crucial. We're known by our work, and when people see Unitarian Universalism, oftentimes that is by the work of community ministers.

What encouragement, advice, or warnings would you give to ministers considering a call outside the parish?

In terms of encouragement, I would say that if you're creative and want a bigger-picture balcony view of the faith tradition, then community ministry is a good fit, though I think the jobs are harder to find in community ministry. You have to be super creative and sometimes entrepreneurial. I lucked out because this job opened up at the time I was looking.

A benefit for me as a person of color is that I don't have to deal with congregations that much. I can deal with religious professionals, which has been way less emotional labor—way less trauma, to be real. There's so much drama for ministers of color, particularly in congregations. If people don't get that, they can read *Centering** and they'll know.

There's so much I miss about parish ministry, especially the family activities. I did a lot of local justice work as a parish minister that I don't really do much of anymore. I don't have the time, but I miss making connections between the church and the community—and planning fun events. I was in charge of a lot of the celebrations at the church, getting to know the kids and families, and accompanying them on the good, the bad, and ugly of their daily lives. That's such a privilege that you don't get in any other role. But I'm also enjoying the peace of mind that I get doing this organizational work. I don't have to worry about a big donor complaining and my job being at risk.

---

* Editor's note: *Centering: Navigating Race, Power, and Authenticity in Ministry* addresses the challenges that religious leaders of color face in exercising agency in a majority white denomination.

Answering the Call of Purposed Peace

Rev. Denise Graves

I see community ministers as people who notice the need in the community. They know, beyond doubt, that they are called to respond.
For me, that need in community is peace. In the crevasses of my
soul, I know that when all sentient beings live in balance, harmony,
and full-provisioned love, there will be peace. I have longed for that
purposed peace. Peace is not passive; it requires all of us to work for
it. I needed then and need now somebody and everybody to present,
promote, and perpetuate a pleasurable, whole peace.

As a young child in school, I sang "Peace I Ask of Thee Oh
River" by Dr. Gwyneth Walker. I sang it when I was nervous, when
there was a school fight, when Black people were being bitten by
police dogs, and when my friends whose parents picked fruit moved
to the next work location. I longed for something my soul knew but
my body had not experienced enough. Somewhere in my journey, I
learned that even if I won a fight, the universe was not made mate-
rially better. If the fight was physical, winning did not make the

Rev. Denise Graves (she/her) serves as a community pastor, minister of
spiritual intersectionality, antiracist dialogue facilitator, and independent
mediator between police and communities. She is the founder and CEO of
Peace Ministry and Institute.

impact of the assaults on my skin, thoughts, and energy stop hurting. I wanted the promised peace "that surpassed all understanding." I wanted to study war no more. I wanted to lay down my burdens of fear, pain, and disappointment "down by the riverside."

In my church choir, I sang the phrase over and over again, "Whenever the Lord says there will be peace." The title of the song is "Peace Be Still," made famous by the great vocalist Rev. James Cleveland. As we walked in protest of police violence, segregation, and the lack of equal pay for equal work, we chanted, "What do you want? PEACE! When do you want it? NOW!" For me, peace offered relief, restoration, gentle love, kindness, and respected visibility.

I founded Peace Ministry LLC, a community ministry and counseling organization, in the early 1990s. Peace Ministry Institute, the formal training arm for peace discipline study, evolved later because there came a need for formal discipleship, stewardship, and spiritual practice that honored the diversity of congregants.

Peace Ministry formed in response to the Kansas City community's high youth homicide rate in the late 1980s and early 1990s. This community needed twenty-four-hour spiritual presence, peace, revelation, love, and more. My community's youth were in trouble, dying in substantial numbers due to drive-by shootings, suicides, intimidation, and other methods of homicide that included reckless driving, drug overuse, and detachment from their own humanity. Families and youth were left to grieve these deaths alone, traumatized, angry, and afraid. The recurring violence seemed relentless, as did the serial grieving.

In response to these experiences, I created a peace-focused vacation Bible school for teens at a local church as a pilot project. Youth knew more about violence than peace; I wanted to share the power, the ability to do so much more, that peace can bring. The activities included talk circles, meditation, grief counseling, organizing for community change, music, poetry and spoken word, and healing movement. Each day, more teens attended. I would visit their homes and talk with them on the streets and in their schools because there is no place where God is not. A Universal Source is everywhere; therefore I can talk about the creative God, the Source, everywhere I am.

People want to know a Creative Source or God of compassion, ever-present—a God who loves them without biases. These youth were transformed. They transformed their community and that church. I learned that purposed peace requires listening, creativity, partnership, vulnerability, and the willing commitment to evolve for the sake of a whole life.

In 2008, I brought the Peace Ministry to New Orleans as an entrepreneurial community ministry that helps people find and live their purpose. Our tagline is "building relationships that enhance the world." We do our work through many different avenues: life coaching, spiritual counseling, mediation, strategic planning, community organizing, training, and public speaking. Other Peace Ministry partners and I have worked closely with a range of religious communities, including three Unitarian Universalist churches in New Orleans through the Center for Ethical Living and Social Justice Renewal, Buddhist temples, Catholic and Protestant churches, Islamic communities, Indigenous American shamans, and diasporic African spiritual traditions such as Ifá, Akan, and Santería.

I have lived around the country. Each city has its own flavor, language, cultures, and sociopolitical norms passed down through history; living in the Deep South is different than living in urban areas in California, Minnesota, Missouri, or Kansas. There was much to learn, confront, and reflect on about righting generational systemic imbalances and seeding my own perception shifts in order to do important liberation work. I am indebted to Southern Black folk who bore and bear the burden of injustice. I am grateful for those of us who now collectively create power platforms of safety, relevant information sharing, tasty food, and so much more to create change. I cannot separate spiritual formation from practical living. My spiritual living is practical living, and it is ever-unfolding. I am grateful for great informants, healers, partners, comrades, and opponents.

While organizing around expanded health care provisions after the Federal Flood and Hurricane Katrina, I was invited to a meeting in the basement of the First Unitarian Universalist Church of New Orleans, and I saw a list of the Seven Unitarian Universalist Principles on colorful posters on the basement walls. For the first time in five years, I was in a room with white people calling for an end to institutional racism. I watched white people sit silent until and while Black people spoke. This was a demonstration of purposed peace. One must have a place to be, speak, and think without fear or assault.

In those meetings, there were white folk who might have meant well, but they were so deeply rooted in their privilege that they were discounting, marginalizing, and assaulting the very people who held Black Power in place and provided resources for their subsistence. These were times I witnessed white people check other white people on their internalized superiority; I loved it. Somebody else was challenging the injustice of structural and institutional racism, and I wanted a partnership with them. I wanted to share twenty years of grassroots organizing with these risk takers. I wanted to learn new tools, tell my truth with support, and cry tears of grief, anger, and rage with people who could hold space for me as well as hear me.

Next the codirector of the Center for Ethical Living and Social Justice Renewal, Rev. Deanna Vandiver, spoke about her experience with the People's Institute for Survival and Beyond, an antiracism education and dialogue experience which allowed her to more deeply face white complicity with injustice. Our work together provided opportunities to redefine how complicity with social norms manifested as internalized inferiority and superiority. As a Black clergy person educated in white institutions, I had internalized harmful and incorrect societal messages about how Black people ought to look, behave, and speak to stay alive that fostered a sense of my own inferiority. These messages were challenged at home, in Deep South cultural faith communities, and in African rituals and practices from Benin and Nigeria.

Along the way, I would see UU people at protest rallies, Black Lives Matters lay-ins, and Take 'Em Down NOLA events. These same people heard sermons about the impact of marginalization and the power of symbols and their reinforcement of outdated values and practices. I listened to stories and jointly created strategies for change. I repeatedly heard Colleen, an antiracist dialogue facilitator, preface her statements with "as a mother of white sons who will become men, I work to develop a different narrative from the superiority of patriarchy and white supremacy." I appreciated her company on the journey, and I also wondered how any white male could avoid the seduction, allure, and rewards of white supremacy and patriarchy. How could these young men demand to be treated the same way someone Black would have been treated for the same infraction of walking while Black, driving while Black, or just minding one's own business while Black? While sitting in small groups of their peers, I heard very different conversations where leveraging occurred on behalf of marginalized Black life. The seduction of privilege was and is often quite compelling, yet there are people who do not surrender to its allure.

Becoming a part of the antiracism dialogues scheduled and facilitated by the Center for Ethical Living and Social Justice Renewal brought me closer to my deeper soul expression: purposed peace. There cannot be peace when our humanity is ignored and devalued. There cannot be peace when only elite whites determine the expression and experience of peace based upon their continuing comfort, power, and maintenance of abundance.

As a spiritual leader, I seek to uncover, exude, promote, and *be* peace. As the spiritual leader of Peace Ministry and Institute, I say that I "purpose peace." This means that on a typical day, I go to the historic and sacred Congo Square in Louis Armstrong Park just across the street from a transitional house for homeless teens and young folk to hold individual appointments, prayer, and meditation circles. I offer presence, "I see you" conversations, prayers, hugs, resources, and consistent demonstration of love-powered peace. Upon invitation, I attend queer and nonbinary gathering spaces, where I share soothing energy, trigger management, meditation, and prayer. I serve as elder counsel to the conveners and participants. In these moments, I have learned more about the harmfulness of my own impulse to assume other people's genders and of the impact of lofty "there is no gender" language in my own life.

These growth moments consistently move me beyond my comfort zone. I have come to realize that we all exist in frames imposed by others, frames we often don't even recognize until we make a misstep and hurt someone. Then we can either stay within the frame or work to expand it—and ourselves.

Asserting that each of us are spiritual leaders, often without a title, is conscious recognition. This recognition is quietly freeing for me, releasing me from overexplaining my claimed identity. What is most important to convey is that each person is seen in their full divinity and gender fluidity as whole. To assert that someone is following your life example, with or without your permission, requires an ability to be in the enough-ness of each and every moment of their and our lives.

As a community minister focused on peace work in a world that celebrates and reports on violence above all other options, I take the responsibility seriously, considering which leaders I follow to influence my own spiritual life. I hold close the inspiration and work of Rev. Dr. Martin Luther King, Jr, who gave us language to understand the ideal of a beloved community—one where all people belong equally, with no exclusivity. I center Sojourner Truth's legal skills and Black woman's humanity and femininity in the center of all discussions about women's rights. I admire Representative Barbara Jordan for her profound political justice verbosity. I stand on the shoulders of Dr. Gloria Scott for giving Black girls space in the public leadership development opportunities provided in the Girl Scouts, an organization I was excluded from as a child. I will always yield to the courageous liberation sense of Fannie Lou Hamer with regard to land ownership, healthy food growth, and Black farmer protections. Her brazen rebellion against murderous racism and economic jealousy changed the course of Black people's voting access and entry into American political leadership after the Reconstruction era.

I will forever tell the truth in print to hold America accountable for what it promotes about life, liberty, and the pursuit of happiness. For Ida B. Wells and countless others, I will chronicle our lives our way. These witnesses charted new courses for adaptive principles and value-based spirituality. I am a product of these great ones introduced to me by Mildred Louise Graves, my mother of eight children. I am my mother's spiritual and justice legacy.

Peace Ministry LLC and Institute is reimagining its purpose to include virtual education, community meditation, community stress reduction, and prayer support, as well as weekly fellowshipping. We also hope to institute a confidential twenty-four-hour prayer line with multispiritual and multilingual faith leadership; there is a need for middle-of-the-night support, as one caller stated, "Once leaving prison and sleeping in my own bed, my nightmares are still real.

Having someone who is nonjudgmental to call would help a lot." Peace Ministry Institute offers certified spiritual leadership coaching classes to assist with this goal of sound spiritual leadership for and by ordinary people. This includes provision of completion certificates and regularly scheduled alumni group meetings to facilitate continuous growth and relationship building.

People on our Monday prayer call report that adjusting from prison life, addictions, and illness is hard. My own life journey included spending time in hospitals, prayer rooms, all-night healing services, healing tents, and more. It included moving around the country so that a single parent of eight could provide for her family. It included quitting school in ninth grade to work full-time to help pay bills. It included lying about my age to work a job in the summer to help take care of our family. I can relate to tough times.

The journey has been arduous, working two jobs, parenting my two younger siblings, and taking a full load of classes to complete a master's degree in public administration as well as teaching at a local church and Youth for Christ while in college. It was all on purpose. Even parenting seven children as the only adult in the household while running a community-based after-school program was on purpose. During the multiple seminary-tour revelations while in Native American sweat lodges, monastery meditation retreats, wilderness adventure activities, and sitting in courtrooms, questioning who these laws were written for, I found myself. I found myself through the smoke of peace pipes, detox and cleansing rituals, intentional silence excursions, and crowded African cities. I found myself and loved her furiously while serving as a community pastor.

One of the things I have learned about spiritual leadership is that there will be scars. There will be moments when your faith is assessed. There will be moments when you need God or something larger than yourself, and it is not Sunday.

It is for those times that I was bred to be a spiritual leader. Every life experience had purpose. I am called to be where people are—on the highways and byways. I am called to community ministry. My hope is that each of us are called to a measure of purposed peace. This world really needs it.

Community Ministry Resources

Community ministry is, by definition, work to be done not alone but in community, in relationship. A host of organizations and resources exist to support Unitarian Universalist ministers as a whole, including community ministers, religious professionals, and laypeople in religious leadership.

Many community ministers belong to multiple professional organizations depending on the type of work they are doing and their personal and professional identities. Some examples include the Association for Unitarian Universalist Music Ministries, Liberal Religious Educators Association, and Transgender Religious professional UUs Together. This book also includes contributions from community ministers involved with Black Lives of UU, EqUUal Access, DRUUMM, and more. My hope is that wherever you are on your journey, you find the UU communities and organizations that nourish your spirit and provide trusted wisdom for your path.

Two organizations that provide particular assistance to community ministers are the UU Society for Community Ministries and the Unitarian Universalist Ministers Association.

The **Unitarian Universalist Society for Community Ministries** (UUSCM) defines itself as a Unitarian Universalist movement of lay ministers and ordained clergy committed to promoting a broad spectrum of healing and social justice ministries. The UUSCM states: "We believe that only through many diverse forms of ministry can we heal the broken, create justice, and live in harmony with the spirit of life. We hold a vision of a larger ministry that sees the world as its parish." UUSCM is unique in that it is a professional organization for both ordained and lay community ministers. Its website provides resources and guidelines for community ministry, including a code of practice and guide to best practices.

The UUSCM offers guidance for writing a covenant between community ministers and congregations. Those covenants guide the relationship between community ministers and the congregations with which they affiliate, including what support community ministers provide to the congregation and vice versa, and how the community and parish ministers honor each other's ministries and boundaries. Please see two examples provided after this section.

UUSCM offers a **Commissioned Lay Ministry** program, where a congregation recognizes an individual's lay ministry as an extension of the ministry of the congregation. Some Commissioned Lay Ministers serve their congregations directly with parish work, others engage in ministry in the larger community. While Commissioned Lay Community Ministers can only be commissioned by a congregation, guidance, support and resources are available from UUSCM.

In 2021, the UUSCM and UUA Ministries and Faith Development office announced a new process for Unitarian Universalists who are seeking faith endorsement for the Board of Chaplaincy Certification Inc (BCCI). This is a track for Unitarian Universalists whose primary interest is chaplaincy and who do not currently desire to become an ordained and fellowshipped minister. The program's goal is "to provide an accountable and accessible process for Unitarian Universalists to pursue a chaplaincy career."

At the time of printing, UUSCM holds First Friday Salons, a monthly gathering of lay and ordained community ministers, on the first Friday of the month, 4 p.m. Central time on Zoom. More information on all of these programs and supports can be found at uuscm.org.

The Unitarian Universalist Ministers Association (UUMA) serves ordained UU ministers and candidates for UU ministry. In 2020, the UUMA added a chapter specifically for community ministers. Its website offers a wealth of resources for UU ministers and those in the process of becoming UU ministers, including coaching, mentoring, professional development, conferences, regional chapters, and newsletters. A key program is the UUMA's Good Offices, which provides support when ministers are in tension or conflict with each other, the institutions they serve, or Unitarian Universalism as a whole.

UUMA.org states, "The Good Officer helps us apply the accumulated wisdom of the liberal ministerial tradition, as articulated in the Guidelines, to our conflict. Lofty and abstract goals, like 'supporting each other's ministries,' take on flesh and blood in these conflicts. The Good Officer helps us navigate these situations, holding us accountable to the high standards of our ministerial tradition in all aspects of our lives. The Good Officer is there when painful and difficult conversations must happen." For more information on Good Offices and UUMA other programs and support for ministers, including community ministers, see UUMA.org.

UU Professional Organizations

Association for Unitarian Universalist Music Ministries (AUUMM): auumm.org

Black Lives of UU (BLUU): blacklivesuu.org

Diverse Revolutionary Unitarian Universalist Multicultural Ministries (DRUUMM): druumm.org

EqUUal Access: equualaccess.org

Liberal Religious Educators Association (LREDA): lreda.org
Transgender Religious professional UUs Together (TRUUsT): transuu.org

Unitarian Universalist Ministers Association (UUMA): uuma.org
Unitarian Universalist Society for Community Ministries (UUSCM): uuscm.org

Sample Covenants

Unitarian Universalism is a covenantal faith. This applies not only to congregants' relationships to and with their congregations but to the ways that ministers and seminarians do their work in relationship to each other. Community ministers benefit from having both an agreement with their congregation and a covenant with the parish minister and any other ministers, seminarians, and staff in the church community. The ministers and congregations below have generously shared their covenants as examples. More can be found on UUSCM.org. For further support, you can reach out to UUMA and request a good officer.

Covenant among Ministers and Seminarians at Unitarian Universalist Congregation at Montclair, New Jersey

Because we recognize that the office of ministry affords power and privilege, and because we recognize our capacity to use our power and privilege for appropriate or inappropriate ends, and because we have been called or hired to together serve a single congregation or called to membership with this congregation, we: covenant to work together to appropriately and honorably fulfill our ministry to the congregation, to the community, to larger circles of Unitarian Universalism, and to the world; and we covenant to build and support a religious community that honors, upholds, and loves its constituents without exception. In service to these aims, in relationship with that which we understand as holy, we covenant, in accordance with the UUMA Guidelines:

✦ To conduct ourselves with integrity, honoring the trust placed in us;

✦ To embody in our lives the values that we proclaim on behalf of our faith;

✦ To support one another in collegial respect and care, understanding and honoring the diversity within our association;

✦ To hold ourselves accountable to each other for the competent exercise of our vocation;

✦ To use our power constructively and with intention, mindful of our potential unconsciously to perpetuate systems of oppression;

✦ To seek justice and right relations according to our evolving collective wisdom, and to refrain from all abuse or exploitation;

✦ To cultivate practices of deepening awareness, understanding, humility, and commitment to our ideals;

✦ To labor earnestly together for the well-being of our communities and the progress of Unitarian Universalism.

Also, in service to these aims, and in awareness of our integrated service to our congregation, we covenant:

✦ To anticipate one another's best intentions with awareness that impact and intention are not always in alignment.

✦ To model right relationship.

✦ To speak with one another, honestly and openly, respecting appropriate boundaries.

✦ To embody a collegial spirit, aware of our shared and integrated dedication to our constituents.

✦ To openly and respectfully consider and move through or beyond disagreements.

✦ To celebrate one another's successes.

✦ To avoid triangulated relationships by dealing directly with persons or groups and by referring persons or groups to one another as appropriate.

✦ To avoid holding confidentiality when doing so would put one another's ministry at risk.

✦ To share information pertaining to one another's ministry with one another before sharing it with the congregation or its constituents.

✦ To set aside regular meeting times, appropriate to the scale and scope of the interrelatedness of our ministries. Suggested:

    ✦ Check-ins with all ministers in the beginning and in the close of the congregational year.

    ✦ Weekly check-ins for all onsite ministerial staff.

Also in service to these aims, and in awareness of the different nature of our particular service to our congregation, we covenant:

✦ To respect the primary role of the senior coministers in setting with the congregation its mission and vision, and in determining with the congregation the means to achieve that mission and vision.

✦ To defer responding to invitations to service or leadership until consulting with the senior ministers.

✦ To acknowledge the reality of the specific and unique power that we each hold informally and to avoid using this informal power to influence the congregation or its constituents in any way inconsistent with the leadership of the other ministers.

✦ To hold the welfare of the congregation as our primary responsibility, individually and collectively.

Review and Amendments

This covenant will be reviewed annually by all the professional ministers and by the Committee on Ministry. Amendments to the covenant can be proposed by the Committee on Ministry or by the professional ministers, but only the professional ministers are authorized to amend the covenant. This covenant will also be reviewed and amended when professional ministers arrive or depart their service to UUCM.

Covenant of Affiliation between Unitarian Church of Hinsdale (UCH) and Affiliated Community Minister

According to UUMA Guidelines, "Community ministers are urged formally to affiliate with a congregation in order to ground themselves in the support and accountability of a Unitarian Universalist covenantal community." In that spirit, we enter into the following covenant:

I. **Overall Relationship.** Rev.'s primary ministry and accountability is as director of the Unitarian Universalist Prison Ministries of Illinois (UUPMI), and UCH supports and affirms this ministry as an extension of its own ministry. Rev. _____ will seek to further UCH's mission, particularly in the area of social justice leadership, and will maintain active, pledging membership in the UCH community. Like all members, they/she/he may participate in congregation activities of her choosing but is under no obligation to do so. They/she/he will not serve in any elected position in the congregation.

II. **Relationship with Minister.** The UUMA Code of Professional Practice shall be carefully observed by Rev. _____ and the UCH minister. As a community minister, Rev. _____

will also abide by the UUSCM Code of Professional Practice. Working collaboratively in a spirit of mutual cooperation and consultation, they/she/he will respect the leadership, relationships, and spheres of responsibility of the UCH minister, and the UCH minister will respect the calling, strengths, and sensibilities of Rev. _____.

III. **Ministerial Role and Tasks.** As an affiliated community minister, Rev. ___ is not employed by nor paid by the congregation on any continuing basis. She will engage the congregation at least twice a year without compensation through preaching, teaching, and support of the Service to Serve, with the understanding that a special offering will be taken yearly for the work of UUPMI. They/she/he may also consult with staff and lay leadership or provide other services in the area of social justice, as invited to do so, without compensation. At the request of the minister, they/she/he may perform other ministerial functions, but is under no obligation to do so. Rev. _____ will take care to defer accepting from members and friends of the congregation any invitation for services properly associated with the ministry of the minister or staff.

IV. **Committee on Shared Ministry.** UCH will empower members to sit on a Committee on Shared Ministry (CoSM). The CoSM will meet with Rev. _____ to provide reflection on activities within the church. This committee will also assist in reviewing the minister for fellowshipping purposes.

V. **Facilities, Supplies, Equipment.** Rev. _____ will retain a key to the UCH office and may have reasonable use of supplies and equipment (paper, photocopier, computer, etc.) without charge for activities related to their/her/his community ministry, including meeting space when available.

VI. **Reporting and Communication.** Rev. ____ will report activity to the minister and will review the relationship with one another and their respective ministries within the life of the congregation. Rev. ____ will keep the congregation informed about the activities of their/her/his ministry via the Annual Report to the congregation and other means as requested.

VII. **Representation of UCH.** Rev. ____ will not speak on behalf of UCH in the absence of a clear prior understanding with the minister and board chair as needed.

VIII. **UCH's Relationship with UUPMI.** Like all UU congregations, UCH may participate in particular UUPMI activities but is under no obligation to do so. Positions taken by UUPMI will in no way be used to imply the endorsement of UCH.

IX. **Addressing Conflict.** Should Rev. ___ and any of the other minister or staff be in conflict, they will seek first the services of a UUMA good officer.

X. **Revisions to this Document.** Changes in this document may be made by agreement between the ministers concerned, and will be effective thirty days after written notice is given to the Board of Trustees, unless the Board votes to delay or reject the changes.

XI. **Termination of Affiliation.** The community minister may resign upon thirty days' notice. The community minister's relationship with the congregation may be terminated upon thirty days' notice by either the senior minister or the Board of Trustees.

_____, UCH Minister

_____, UCH Board President

Rev. _____, Affiliated Community Minister

Acknowledgments

Thank you so much to the contributors to this book for their wisdom, patience, and generous spirits, and to Mary Benard at Skinner House for being with us all along the way. Abundant, heart-singing, feet-dancing love to my family, my bandmates in Parker Woodland and Butch County, the S.A. Crew, the Zumbies, the YMCA of Austin, especially Jude Hickey and my committees on ministry, Wildflower Church in Austin, Texas, and all the congregations who had me as a guest in their pulpit during the pandemic. To Deanna Vandiver, Brian Ferguson, Marisol Caballero, the Central Texas UU Ministers cluster, Simone Barnes, Eileen Flynn, Amy Markley, and my Meadville Lombard colleagues. To Meg Barnhouse for being the first female minister who encouraged me and the first one I saw in the pulpit with a guitar.

Fierce love to everyone doing the daily work of justice and liberation, especially everyone involved with the Texas UU Justice Ministry, and to all the musicians, writers, and ministers who get me through. And again, to my family, extended and chosen, and especially the grandparents, siblings, and the ones I call home: Patrick, Ace, and David. I love you infinity.